Latino Young Men and Boys in Search of Justice

Testimonies

Latino Young Men and Boys in Search of Justice

Testimonies

EDITED BY
Frank de Jesús Acosta

CO-EDITED
Henry A. J. Ramos

FOREWORD
Luis J. Rodríguez, Author of *Always Running*

Arte Público Press
Houston, Texas

Latino Young Men and Boys in Search of Justice is funded in part by grants from The California Endowment, California Community Foundation, Marguerite Casey Foundation, City of Houston through the Houston Arts Alliance, W. K. Kellogg Foundation and the Sierra Health Foundation. We are grateful for their support.

Recovering the past, creating the future

Arte Público Press
University of Houston
4902 Gulf Fwy, Bldg 19, Rm 100
Houston, Texas 77204-2004

Cover art by Alberto Symon
Cover design by Mora Des!gn

Names: Jesús Acosta, Frank de, editor. | Ramos, Henry A. J., 1959- editor.
    Title: Latino young men and boys in search of justice : testimonies / edited by Frank de Jesus Acosta and Henry A. J. Ramos ; foreword: Luis J. Rodriguez, Author of Always Running.
    Description: Houston, TX : Arte Publico Press, 2016.
    Identifiers: LCCN 2015025479 | ISBN 9781558858213 (alk. paper)
    Subjects: LCSH: Juvenile justice, Administration of—United States. | Hispanic American youth—United States. | Juvenile delinquency—United States.
    Classification: LCC HV9104 .L327 2016 | DDC 364.36089/68073—dc23
    LC record available at http://lccn.loc.gov/2015025479
                                                                    CIP

♾ The paper used in this publication meets the requirements of the American National Standard for Information Sciences—Permanence of Paper for Printed Library Materials, ANSI Z39.48-1984.

15 16 17 18 19 20   9 8 7 6 5 4 3 2 1

Table of Contents

Raza Cósmica: Barrio and Pinto Arte, Community Mural Projects and Cultura Tattoo Arts

Acknowledgements

Our undying gratitude and appreciation for the support, partnership, leadership, contributions, friendship, love and prayers of those who made this publication and community education project possible. Particularly, Dr. Nicolás Kanellos, Dr. Gabriela Baeza Ventura, Dr. Gail C. Christopher, Luz E. Benítez Delgado, Dr. Robert K. Ross, Luz Vega-Marquis, Robert Phillips, Antonia Hernández, Nike Irvin, Peter Rivera, Charles Fields, Beatriz Solís, Ray Colmenar and Michael Palumbo (Graduate Fellow and Advisor).

We especially wish to acknowledge our institutional partners and supporters: namely, our publishers and project sponsors Arte Público Press at the University of Houston and the Insight Center for Community Economic Development, as well as our funders: The California Endowment, Marguerite Casey Foundation, W. K. Kellogg Foundation and the Sierra Health Foundation.

We could not have found such powerful creative voices and works to feature here without the incredible work and goodwill of our organizational partners and their committed staff: The National Compadres Network, Santa Cruz Barrios Unidos, Communities United for Restorative Youth Justice, Tía Chucha's Centro Cultural and Bookstore, Homies Unidos, Catholic Prison Ministries/Healing Justice Coalition, La Plazita Institute, Homeboy Industries, Policy Link, the Gathering for Justice and Inside Out Writers (Leslie Poston). Arte Público Press (Nellie Gonzales and Matthew Hall); The Insight Center for Community Economic Development (Michael Palumbo and Brad Caftel); CURYJ (Freddy Gutiérrez, Michael Muscadine,

José Luis Pavón, Rubén Leal, and Rana Halpern); Santa Cruz Barrios Unidos (Cynthia Gutiérrez, Jennifer Barajas, Fátima RodríguezOrtiz and Edgar Puga).

We gratefully acknowledge the valued assistance of our impressive council of project advisors: Jerry Tello, Luis J. Rodríguez, Nane Alejandrez, Father Greg Boyle, Rubén Lizardo, Richard Montoya, George Galvis, Albino García, Jr., Alex Sánchez, Javier Stauring, Carmen Pérez, Luis Cardona and Tomás Alejo.

Additionally, we express special gratitude to our personal circle of loving support and creative inspiration: María Acosta, Luis García, Claudia Lenschen-Ramos, Gregory Ramos, Kiki Ramos Gindler, José Fonseca, Alejandro Delgadillo, Pat Shibuya, Jerry Tello, Donald and Tawnya, Bill Bamish, John Palumbo, Otilio Quintero, Henry Domínguez, Arturo Ybarra, Gary and Nancy Kobayashi, Peter Nishita, Linda Bowen, Dr. Guadalupe Rivera Marín, Evangeline Ordáz and Armando Molina, Lorraine García-Nakata, Anne Laddon, Sasha Irving, Mary Legleiter, Mariano and Ruby Díaz; and Carmen, Joe, Cecilia and Henry, Ronnie, Yvette, Michael and Willie A, Jojo, Roz and Mark, Familia Fonseca; and Rolling Stone, Katie, Anthony, Michael, Marc, Johnny, Lisa, Anthony, Christopher, Daniela, Mariano Jr. "Pops" and Jason; Spirit Relations—Cecilia Sandoval, Michael Balaoing, Richard Verches, Blanca Almeida, Bong Hwan Kim, Debbie Ching, Stewart Kwoh, Connie Rice, Sandra Gutiérrez, Tom David, Gabby Gonzales, Ramón Miramontes, Albesa Ybarra, Blair Chambers, Rubén and Sarah Gonzales, Sally Lew, Antonio Manning, Angel Zapata, John Castillo, Marvin Thurman, Mike López, Benny Torres, Vusi, Mandla, Fran Jemmott, Gaylord, Shedrick, Venice, Jitu Sadiki, Anthony Alejandrez and Magdalena Beltrán del Olmo; Barrio Whittier (Patrick Irish, Paul-Mick-Matt, Jessie and Carol, Metz, Limon, Klein, Kiko, Tocayo Frank, John Q & V, Skip, Cholo Pat, Bobby, Yvonne, Victor P, the JTS and Tubby's gang. Rest in Peace Papa John Palumbo, Helen Verches, Esperanza Lizardo and John Caldwell, who passed to the spirit world during the becoming of this book.

In Loving Memory of José Montoya

This book is dedicated to Movimiento Warrior Poet, maestro José Montoya. José passed into the spirit world in September 2013. He was truly one of the seminal activist-artists, muralists, poets, writers, musicians and educators who used their gifts in the cultural arts to advance freedom, the struggle for justice, pluralism and human dignity for Chicano, Latino and Indigenous people.

Frank de Jesús Acosta

"José Montoya—poet, painter, community organizer, educator, leading Chicano rights advocate and agent provocateur—died September 25, 2013 at the age of 81, leaving a formidable legacy of art and activism. The *Sacramento Bee*'s obituary called him 'one of the most influential and inspirational figures in California Latino history.'

"Every movement has its intellectuals—the poets, writers and academics crucial to shaping and articulating a people's identity while the political winds swirl and the world becomes dangerous. José Montoya was a cultural front-liner and first responder—a doer; a creator who brought levity, defiance and satirical wit to the bloody fields of the San Joaquin Valley as well as to the frigid halls of academe, all the way to the state capitol and beyond. In the political tumult of the 60s and 70s, José led a pack of sacred clowns, profane and profound poets, dedicated artists who brushed up against the San Joaquin

County Sheriff deputies and the bloody fists of Teamsters who were muscle for ranchers. Yet our father and his merry band of deadly serious artists strictly adhered to [César] Chávez's unyielding demand for a nonviolent movement. That message didn't make it to everyone at the time, and I saw our father disarm many a young man or Brown Beret.

"That was José, a man fit and locked into his times, marching to an improvised drumbeat, always loyal to César while writing elegant poetry that anchored the Chicano movement. José was never afraid of hard work; he instilled this ethic into each of us, an ethic born of his post-Depression era upbringing, pulled into sharp focus from the cotton fields of Bakersfield to the vineyards of Fowler. In his landmark poem 'El Sol y los de Abajo,' he relished the idea of casting himself as a lackluster farmworker, while his family was known as amazingly fast 50-tray-a-day grape pickers:

How I was easy on the clusters
Preferring instead to allow

The iridescent worm live in that leafy green world

"José was always humanizing the common farmworker and his workplace, his master strokes on par with his heroes, Steinbeck and Saroyan. He was also a committed multiculturalist. Dad was a hugely public man who still gave us our precious, private family time while the world was inflamed by the assassinations of MLK and RFK. We saw monumental selflessness and generosity from a man who had huge demands placed on him and who answered for many people. José was a rock star, but always a dad, imperfect like all fathers, but with a heart so huge it still beats and flows like the rivers he loved: the American, the Feather, the Kings y su río El Sacramento. . . . He was raising children, lots of them, always providing, with our mom, for a large and growing brood of hungry Montoyas, while innovating art activism and education.

"José did it, man. He gave, he taught and he professed until the end. He crossed that finish line bravely, fighting a relentless foe, teaching us until his last breath, the public man ultimately succumbing, but always a glimmer in his eye, a will to live, a look that said if anybody could outsmart this disease it would be this Chicano trickster. We quietly strummed a Mexican corrido on his legendary guitar. José seemed to be mounting a colt from his New Mexico youth. And then the final breaths came—three long poetic breaths to last a life-time. A breath: like a poem or a book of humility. Another breath: a book of courage. The final breath: a book of surren-der and dignity. We lovingly and carefully carried our father, José E. Montoya, out of his famous home on D Street, the sur-viving members of his beloved Royal Chicano Air Force assembled and lining the walkway from his steps to the street where the hearse waited. The Chicano General was given a full and final salute to the quiet refrains of 'De Colores.' A small white United Farm Workers flag was gently placed over his heart; he was united with his homeboy César once again. Fireworks were detonated into the dark sky, and even the cops rolled by, but José Montoya, existential icon, poet, artist, hus-band, brother, teacher, father and, yes, Chicano intellectual romantic, was long gone. A single candle flickered in his liv-ing room window through the night for all of Sacramento to see from the streets he loved and sketched and wrote about. Only the words from his epic pachuco poem 'El Louie' seemed fitting now: ' . . . his life had been remarkable, un vato de atolle.'"

Richard Montoya, *Sacrament Bee*, October 13, 2013

El Pueblo's Poet Laureate
(José Montoya, ¡Presente!)

Frank de Jesús Acosta

Beautiful heart of the spirit warrior
Lifetime of loving, creativity, sacrifice
In the twilight of your journey; only grace
Malady could not deny a last sweet sunset
Smiling upon the harvest of your milpa
Surrounded by grateful flowers

Tu familia, amistades, el pueblo de tu corazón
Warrior, maestro, composer of human poetry
Artista's flor y canto gave us tapestries of life
Colors of justice, songs of hope, the call to action
Litanies of nuestra historia, cultura cura y destino
Chicanismo; beauty and belonging to la Raza Cósmica

Pueblo's prayer of love brought you to the crossroads
Supplications to Tata Dios, Ometeotl, la Virgen
Farewell scenes of reminiscence; reckoning; veneration
We offer ceremonies of gratitude and peaceful passage
The pueblo's poet laureate draws his last three breaths
Sweet sunset of courage, dignity, humility; eternal harvest of love

PREFACE
La Cultura Cura (Healing Culture)
Frank de Jesús Acosta and Henry A. J. Ramos

Poetry and Arte is eternal soul speak, heart to heart, imagination to imagination, spirit to spirit; imparting what academic rigor and science by themselves cannot express of love, truth, experience, profound beauty, transformative pain, the power of forgiveness, dignity, frailty, humanity, faith or the most sacred visions in our journey . . .

—Frank de Jesús Acosta

For decades, California's social, economic and political landscape has produced large numbers of Latino young men and boys whose normal and healthy development has been stifled, if not suspended. Beginning with their early experiences in families that often are under severe economic (and, owing in many instances to non-citizenship status, political) hardship, most of these young Americans face great disadvantages before they even have the opportunity to reach adulthood.

Everywhere Latino young men and boys go, they face largely unresponsive educational institutions, discriminatory employers and intensely hostile law enforcement agencies. There is little doubt that these young people have been subjected to detrimental barriers to success in American society. The eventual manifestations and consequences of these adversities are predictably troubling and tragic: gangbanging, crime, violence, addiction and, in many cases, early death.

For still too many Californians (and others across the nation), the perennial association of young Latino men and boys with these pathologies seems uneventful, unsurprising, not newsworthy. To many, Latino youth themselves, and their families by extension, are primarily responsible for their own demise. If they are poor, it is seen as being a reflection of their laziness or lack of initiative. If they are in trouble with the law, it is understood to be a matter of bad decision-making and criminal disposition. If they cannot succeed in school, it is seen as an indication of their innate intellectual inferiority.

Sadly, such misperceptions and misunderstandings of reality—particularly in the context of hard economic times like these—play a still-too-prevalent role in public policy processes that establish the rights and opportunities of various minorities in society. As a result, over the past decades (with only recent signs of relief, as in the November 2014 passage of Proposition 47, which invoked the important Three Strikes Law sentencing reforms for offenders), California and other states have experienced an unprecedented push from legislators and policy makers to criminalize Latinos and other youth of color. This has occurred now to the point where Latino young men and boys are more likely to go to prison than to graduate from college. Most active Latino youth and young adult offenders are also more likely to die prematurely from gang or gang-related violence than from natural causes.

From an obscured amalgamation of stereotype and fact, many outsiders who observe the plight of Latino youth simply see them as inherently bad apples—so bad that seeking to redeem or otherwise reclaim them is futile. To an extreme few still, these young men and boys really should be considered more like animals or things, rather than humans.

But the grim data and harsh narratives that often go with them belie another story. They gloss over a much brighter side of the equation, which is the uplifting possibility of what even the most gang-hardened Latino young men and boys can become if we and others like us encourage and support them in a more positive direction.

It turns out that Latino men and boys—including even the most gang- and crime-tested among them—are full of the same kinds of hopes, dreams and desires the rest of us hold within. They have similar passions, similar fears and similar needs. They have the same kinds of attributes that make all of us—whatever our station or background—human.

Nothing reveals our humanity in life like creative expression. The arts are so powerful precisely because they cut through the anonymity of our commercial transactions and material acquisitions—as well as the growing rancor and divisiveness of our public discourse—to remind us more about what we share in common rather than what divides us.

Though too often perversely monetized and rendered elitist in our modern society, the arts are inherently democratic. They give a stage to any idea or form that can find its way into the public realm, however it gets there and by whoever can produce it. When properly activated, the arts can be a ready tool for even the least endowed among us; hence their appeal to the young, the disenfranchised and the alternative in societal position and perspective.

These properties make resorting to creative expression particularly accessible and appealing to Latino young men and boys, who are part of a now well-established, multigenerational tradition of graffiti-based creative culture that found its legs in the early 1970s through mural art and that now carries forward not only in the form of graffiti and tattoo art, but also poetry, first-person prose, multi-media expressive works and the performing arts.

The pages that follow reflect the incipient elements of an important new virtual center for artistic and creative expression that is being established for Latino men and boys by Arte Público Press at the University of Houston. Its development, in partnership with the Insight Center for Community Economic Development, and funding from The California Endowment, Marguerite Casey Foundation, W. K. Kellogg Foundation, California Community Foundation and the Sierra Health Foundation, will encourage the posting, curation and interactive discussion of original works by Latino men and boys in California and elsewhere across the nation as they illustrate the conditions these young people face and the visions they hold for a better future.

We hope that by establishing this unprecedented space for the creative and expressive exchange of Latino men and boys, we can illuminate the common elements of these young peoples' humanity, their analyses of the circumstances they face, and suggest solutions in policy and practice that, if pursued, would help to improve the conditions and life prospects of these young Americans.

While initially focused on the California experience, we hope over time to cultivate this platform to establish a more broad based national repository of Latino men's and boys' creative voice, along with supporting content and commentary (both written and videographic), that can help to put American law and culture on a more intelligent and sustainable path relative to the full utilization of Latino men's and boys' capacities in American culture, economy and public policy.

We are grateful to Nicolás Kanellos, Founder and Director of Arte Público Press (APP), for his visionary support of our work, which dates back to his encouraging our earlier 2007 collaboration. That partnership, in turn, lead to a published history and commentary on the work of Santa Cruz, CA-based Barrios Unidos—a trailblazer in this space, building on commentaries by national luminaries ranging from actor and social justice activist Harry Belafonte and United Farm Workers Union co-founder Dolores Huerta, to former anti-war activist and California legislator Tom Hayden and award-winning writer and poet Luis J. Rodríguez.

For this current project, we are especially indebted to allied community partners whose frontline work to support Latino men and boys has been defining, both in California and elsewhere. These include the leaders of organizations like Barrios Unidos, Communities United for Restorative Youth Justice, Homies Unidos, La Plazita Institute, Homeboy Industries, the Gathering for Justice and National Compadres Network, among others. Their efforts, guidance and support have truly helped to make this effort both possible and worthy.

We encourage you to read and view forward with an eye to gaining a deeper insight into the still-largely-untapped power of Latino men's and boys' creative viewpoints. We urge you to see the world for a moment through their eyes and their hearts. We prompt you to examine your own perceptions and possible latent prejudices relative to young men like these. Lastly, we defy you to find any lack of humanity or purpose in the voices featured throughout.

FOREWORD
How Trouble Becomes the Thread of a Whole and Meaningful Life
Luis J. Rodríguez

I was asked to speak to the root causes of the disproportionate representation of boys and men of color in the justice
system in America; in particular, the representation of Latino
males and important contextual factors specific to this population (e.g., poverty in communities, families, schools, gangs,
trauma of community violence, immigration, cultural identity
and spirituality).

The roots for the disproportionate number of young men of
color in the justice system are economic, political and historical—this includes the vast and growing Latino population. The
main issue facing these populations is poverty. The poor are
largely powerless and moneyless. This often translates to young
men as hopeless, helpless, rootless and eventually (as a summation of all these propensities) meaningless. They are more likely to join gangs, indulge in substance abuse, leave school and/or
work in low-paying, largely undignified jobs. This is true for all
poor, regardless of color. In relation to Latinos of color (i.e.,
black, Native/brown or mixed), they also face discriminatory
barriers based on race, language and immigrant status.

When the United States underwent a historical transition
from industrial production to high tech/digital production in

the 1970s and 1980s, most inner city jobs were sourced out of the country or displaced by robotics. Cynically, a collusion of government, economic and political forces opened the flood-gates to drugs, especially during the period of a "war on drugs" begun under Nixon's presidency and continued with Reagan, although both Democrats and Republicans have sustained this travesty to the present.

At the same time, firearms, including from foreign wars, inundated the urban core of most cities, eventually spreading to suburbs and rural communities. Then civil wars in El Sal-vador and Guatemala in the 1980s—involving U.S. funding and training—led to an influx of refugees as well as from increasingly economically strapped (and politically corrupt) Mexico and Honduras.

With lack of decent paying jobs, the drug trade became the "economic" life in poor and marginal communities, especially those most hit by de-industrialization (e.g., Los Angeles and Chicago, being the most prominent, but also Detroit, Wash-ington D.C., Baltimore, New York City, San Antonio, Phoenix, Albuquerque and others).

These motive forces led to increased gang involvement across the spectrum. In 1980 there were 2,000 gangs with 100,000 members in around 300 cities; today there are an esti-mated 1.5 million gang members in 35,000 gangs in some 5,000 cities and towns. By the numbers, Latinos have more gang-affiliated youth than any other group (disproportionate-ly, African Americans are most active in gangs). Latino gangs include the oldest continuous street gangs among Chicanos in such places as Los Angeles and El Paso, but also Puerto Ricans in New York City and Chicago, as well as more recently arrived Central American/Caribbean refugee youth.

The U.S. government's response has been punitive. The greatest investment in prison building reached its peak in the

1990s (mostly during the Clinton Administration). By 2014 the United States had 25 percent of the world's prisoners, although it is only 5 percent of the world's population.

Today the federal government's budget for the drug war—largely declared a failure by most Americans—is $25 billion, with a third of this going to local law enforcement. Police disproportionately target Black and Latino males (Blacks are four times more likely to get arrested for drug offenses than whites), even as medical and recreational marijuana use has been allowed in California, Colorado, Washington and other states. Again, this is a double standard—the growing legalization of marijuana presently benefits largely well-off white communities, not the poor or black and brown.

As the largest state prison system, California has a $10 billion annual budget. Forty years ago the state had 15,000 prisoners, mostly white, in 15 institutions—today it has 130,000 prisoners in 34 institutions, 70 to 80 percent of color. As Michelle Alexander has written, this is the new "Jim Crow."

Correspondingly, America has adopted some of the most harmful of punitive law enforcement, criminal/juvenile justice policies and practices harming communities of color (e.g., Three Strikes, trying children as adults, Zero Tolerance and School Expulsion policies, Gang Data Bases, Drug and Gang Enhanced Sentencing). These are the result of widely held mainstream fears based on divisive conservative misinformation campaigns, such as the now debunked "Super-Predator Myth." Such myths have created a blanket indictment of presumed criminality for black and brown youth and men, hence giving rise to the context and social values that underlie the present reality.

In Los Angeles, there are now around 40 gang injunctions affecting 70 communities, all black and brown. Gang injunctions arrest whole neighborhoods, where alleged gang members cannot congregate, show tattoos, have cell phones, and must be in their homes at dusk or be subject to police detainment, photographing, database entry and arrest. California implements gang injunctions in mostly areas slated for gentrification. Similar laws exist elsewhere, such as "mob action" in Chicago and "stop-and-frisk" in New York City.

Three-strike laws, gang and gun enhancements, zero tolerance, school removals and such are also used most often against black and brown residents, fueling the massive prison industrial complex. Fear engendered by misinformation continues to be the underlying reason why many voters may still continue to support such measures, even though they have only made gangs stronger and better organized.

Due to the squeezing of urban core communities through punitive measures and gentrification—the re-alignment of wealth back to the city, removing black, brown and poor people, including the tearing down of 1940s federal housing projects—gangs are now spread around the country.

With deportations heightened since the 1990s, U.S.-based gangs, mostly from L.A. and Chicago, are now active in other parts of the world. The most salient is the impact of 700,000 allegedly criminally involved immigrants that since 1996 have been sent back to Mexico, El Salvador, Guatemala and Honduras (the latter countries are known as the Northern Triangle and have the world's highest murder rates)—enough to change local cultures in these countries.

The facts keep proving that more policing and prisons only create more gangs, violence and uncertainty. I contend the bloated prison and drug war budgets have made our communities unsafe. "Tough on crime" doesn't work. It's tougher—and more effective—to care for youth, male and female; to provide help to traumatized communities, broken families; to bring jobs and training to unproductive lives; to expand rehabilitation, drug and mental health treatment, education; to establish healing circles, restorative justice and proper initiatory community-based practices. These are also far less costly.

Certainly, the Latino and Black communities, particularly males, have been harmed by the existing negative racial bias in law enforcement, sentencing and the draconian punishment-focused justice model. The fact is all males are harmed by any negative obstructions to their growth, health and learning. Punitive measures harm people. They have caused a precarious and dangerous environment in this country. When mixed with racial, gender or sexual orientation bias, as well as economic and other barriers, youth are subjected to multiple stressors. Little wonder some of them lose it—become suicidal, addictive, criminals.

People are not animals or numbers. Nobody's humanity or dignity should ever be taken away. Even if a youth has done a horrendous crime, the community (manifested as society, laws and courts, etc.) should hold the ground with lasting principles, maintaining its center and never stooping to being narrow-minded, emotionally wrought adults. I've been in many courts, schools, juvenile lockups and prisons. While there are many upstanding and caring personnel in these institutions, I've also seen emotional outbursts from representatives of courts and institutions, inhumane treatment, subhuman torture (including solitary confinement) and more.

Whatever happened to initiatory practices, rites of passage, mentoring, relationships that last? Whatever happened to resources for those suffering from family abuse, broken schools, neglected communities? People need help; properly helped they become less helpless. We have taken away the power of people to make decisions, influence public policy, to contribute in positive ways. This is often exhibited as less personal power. High expectations require high patience.

Deep disconnection is the main motive force for the growth in school shootings (mostly by white middle-class alienated youth) as well as gangs, dropping out of schools, giving up.

For Latino males these barriers, laws and biases have created "monsters," in the sense of mutated human beings. They can be helped, change is possible, but everything points to losing trust in human capacities; denying the abundant good inherent in people, the power of nurturing relationships and our spiritual nature. America needs a new imagination, a new model, a new cosmology to guide our work with the most troubled youth. Trouble either makes a community or destroys it. What we do makes the difference.

The concept of a "School-to-Prison Pipeline" has been introduced to the national dialogue. The premise is that schools and the institutions of education in impoverished communities have failed, creating the circumstances and/or pathways to prison for young men of color. Dealing with this stark reality is the central focus of President Obama's "My Brother's Keeper" initiative. Reducing the clear racial disparity of educational achievement, incarceration and recidivism rates are MORAL and PRACTICAL imperatives for America.

People have said the present instability and crisis have moral roots. That's true, but mostly because there's a huge gap between what we say and what we do. We are largely a Christian nation, perhaps the most Christian in the developed world, yet we continue to have death penalties; life sentences, including for juveniles; inhumane and sterile electronic prisons; and racial/class biases in convictions and sentencing. We continue to have growing income disparities and injustices. That's the capitalist economy and the system of governance linked to it—not Christianity.

Where's the moral outrage? Most Christians are supportive of such measures, totally at odds with the "what Jesus would do" mantra. The Jesus in the Gospels loved, healed, went up against the rich and powerful, the corrupt and appeased, but we turn away from fourteen-year-olds facing 135 years (I've seen this) and police beatings, killings and abuse of power.

Now among some powerful churches, Jesus is a Republican, a cowboy, a redneck. You don't believe me—in a Waco, Texas cemetery there is statue of Jesus with cowboy boots!

Jesus is not a Republican redneck, but people who lie about their God will lie about anything. We need true Christian values and love, not the ones hi-jacked by the Christian right.

Young people have a built-in B. S. meter. They can see and feel the hypocrisy. They are hungry for authenticity, truth that lasts, meaningful and respectful relationships with adults. While I am no longer a Christian (although raised Catholic), I do live the values of Jesus' "Sermon on the Mount." I also understand the truths expounded by Buddha, Mohammed, Black Elk and others. They all have validity, although I can also discern how people have from time to time misrepresented and misapplied these teachings.

Jesus said it best, as quoted in Matthew 7:12: "So in everything, do to others what you would have them do to you, for this sums up the Law and the Prophets." Even non-Christians can agree. Let's make this both the moral and practical imperatives of our words, actions and law. "On Earth as in Heaven."

Instead, we have man-made illusions like the "free market," "mortgages," "borders" and the wage system, and made them bigger and more sacred than Jesus (or we've forced Jesus' life and teachings into these relatively recent and narrow developments). Even Karl Marx said, "An invitation to abandon illusions about a situation is an invitation to abandon a situation in need of illusions." I'm with the youth—"be real." Consumerism, profits, war, guns, hate—these have become our Gods.

It is a positive development that California and other states are beginning to ask questions about the premise of our juvenile justice system. Communities are organizing to reform what the core values and guiding principles of the criminal and juvenile justice systems in America should be. What should these values and guiding principles be? What does a restorative or holistic justice approach look like?

While banks, corporations, energy companies, high-tech companies can poison the earth; while they can "nickel and dime" us to death; while the one percent can maintain control no matter who is elected; while we can lose our homes, our health and justice; while the rich get richer, the poor get prison; we are told to be compliant, don't rock any boats, to keep shopping.

I can't and I won't.

The criminal justice system is unjust and bloated. Taxpayers are providing "schooling" in prisons—when they don't have programming, rehabilitation or healing—for better-organized and effective criminals. Now gangs are more businesslike, and big businesses have become more like gangs.

Our values should be that trouble in youth is the very material to make a life; that everyone is born with genius; that every person must be allowed to live out their passions, destinies, stories; that abundance is the natural state (while scarcity is man-made and unnatural); that change is constant; that regeneration of people, environment and economies is endemic to whole and connected relationships.

It's about alignment, integrality, wholeness.

These are indigenous ideas, ancient ideas. But they apply under all conditions, even the modern ones. I'm not against progress, development, new technology. I'm against losing our core values as humans, our perennial philosophies, to the most immediate, static and literal ones. We've lost the mythologies, stories and metaphors to teach and direct us.

Imagine a new world where thriving and affirming communities exist everywhere. Imagine changing our values from "dog eat dog," "kill or be killed," or "only the strong survive" to this: The whole and healthy development of anyone is dependent on the whole and healthy development of everyone.

There is growing empirical evidence of the devastating negative impact of the criminal and juvenile justice systems on the life chances of boys and young men of color in America. Prisons and their practical human outcomes make them an institutional arm of preserving a socially, economically and politically marginalized underclass. People often use decreasing budgets as excuses not to implement comprehensive reform and workable strategies. They force austerity measures for the poor and working class: cuts in social programming, food and job access, in arts and creative development. But I counter that it takes more money, more tax dollars, not to do these.

In California I would remove the $10 billion prison budget (it takes $46,000 a year to house an adult; $252,000 a year for a juvenile) and put this money into truly transformative practices, policies and actions. I would end projects like the high-speed rail from Los Angeles to San Francisco that will grow to $220 billion when it's done (and only serve 200,000 mostly business commuters); I would better tax the $38 billion generated in the state's ports, the largest commercial ports in the country. Today California is the only place on the planet that does not have a severance tax for companies who "sever" oil from the land. I would tax the oil companies and at the same time work on clean and renewable energy sources to end our dependence on oil.

I would make education and health care free and with the highest quality. I would make all arts, music, dance, theater and writing more accessible to all people. I would end poverty as well as create clean and green environments for all.

Why not? These are not only possible but also imperative.

The fact is it takes billions of dollars to keep people poor, disenfranchised and in prisons.

The very thing we fear is the very thing we're breeding.

Nationally I would end our war economy—over $2 trillion in Iraq and Afghanistan in the past thirteen years, although our world is more insecure than ever. Instead I would establish a Peace and Healing Economy.

I submit—and many economists and scholars would agree—all of this is incompatible with the profit-based large-scale global capitalist economic/political matrix we live under. We need to imagine another way to go, then methodically and thoroughly go that way.

If people claim that what I'm proposing is bad for business, I'd argue that our high prison rate creates higher crime rates, and poverty creates more broken, unhealthy and unstable people. That's bad for business and everything else. It's good for business to have people with good health, strong jobs, education and growing families. Prosperity for all is best for business. Income inequality and deepening inequities are not.

Lastly, I'd like to speak to the importance of considering the diverse history and rich cultural make-up of the Latino community, where some specific issues, strategies and approaches (e.g., La Cultura Cura; traditional rites of passage; cultural traditions and the arts; spiritual healing; familial community supports) are being reintroduced to communities in order to improve the life chances of Latino males.

I've used healing circles, writing workshops, stories, poems, sweat lodge ceremonies and more in my work with the most troubled youth, mostly Chicano/Central American, but also African American, Puerto Rican, Asian, European and Native American.

Through the Mosaic Multicultural Foundation of Seattle, run by renowned storyteller Michael Meade, I've helped mentor young men, many in gangs, as well as men from all walks of life and races, in conferences addressing issues of genius, mentoring, destiny, rage, addictions, violence and more. We've done Voices of Youth writing workshops with inner-city young people in L.A., Chicago, Seattle and other cities.

I've worked with and mentored organizations like B.U.I.L.D. in Chicago, Homeboy Industries in L.A., Spreading Seeds/Healing Network in L.A. County, Barrios Unidos in Santa Cruz and Hombres & Jóvenes Nobles, among others.

I've also used art, dance, theater, writing, music and such in poor working-class communities with the co-founding of Tía Chucha's Centro Cultural & Bookstore in the Northeast San Fernando Valley and our Young Warriors Project as well as Chicago's Youth Struggling for Survival and Guild Complex, among others. And I've done readings/talks and conferences over the past forty years in prisons, juvenile lockups, migrant camps, housing projects, homeless shelters, Native American Reservations, public and private schools, libraries, colleges and universities across the United States.

In addition, I've taken this work throughout Canada, Mexico, El Salvador, Guatemala, Nicaragua, Peru, Venezuela, Argentina, Puerto Rico, Japan—as well as such European cities as Paris, Berlin, Hamburg, Cologne, Frankfurt, Stuttgart, Heidelberg, Tuebingen, Isny, Salzburg, Amsterdam, Groningin, Rome, Milan, Manchester, London and Sarajevo (including to some of the worst prisons and slums).

For Chicanos/Mexicanos/Central Americans we've linked youth development and gang intervention with ancestral roots and practices by deepening knowledge in the Mexika (so-called Aztec) and Mayan cosmologies, but also with tribal knowledge from the United States and other parts of the hemisphere.

I'm in agreement with La Cultura Cura—where culture, creativity and connection is utilized to balance, harmonize and make whole persons, families and communities previously wrought by the worst aspects of being uprooted, ignored, confused, addictive and raging.

For Latino males the answers are in our hands; the diversity of spiritual practices and lineages allow us to draw from Native, African, Asian and European traditions. The modern "war" against our youth and adult men has to end. We need to be the medicine for a wounded, fractured and unequal world. This means aligning our deepest wisdoms with the most advanced tools and the most cohesive and healthy communities.

Again: imagine this is possible. Then let's organize to make this happen by tapping into the inherent capabilities/ regenerative capacity in human nature and in nature.

Editor's Note

Frank de Jesús Acosta

It was late Fall and I was writing by my neighbors' swimming pool in La Habra Heights, pondering the serendipitous path that brought me to this place in time from *mi rincón del mundo*, the streets of East Los Angeles. I prayed as the sage smoke drifted into the afternoon sky, wafts taking the shape of clouds, memories and faces of the boys and young men of color I had met in the process of writing this book. A feeling of shame came upon me as I wondered why I was spared incarceration, unlike so many of these precious lives.

I thought of the journeys so powerfully expressed in the poems, writings and arte chosen for publication in this book. They are filled with pain, repentance, revelation, healing, transformation and redemption. I thought of those young people still sitting in their prison cells, perhaps one of the darkest journeys a man or women can experience, but still finding a way to live in their higher humanity. There, but for the grace of God, go I. The most serious missteps of my youth involved the smalltime enterprise of weed, something I regrettably dabbled in to survive the shit hole that is poverty.

As I sat alone, free and blessed to be writing under a sweet blue sky, my mind wandered to a crossroads moment that could have easily landed me in prison for many years. The summer after graduating high school I was hanging out with some stoner friends one lazy Friday afternoon. This relatively innocent gathering turned into a weekend binge that lasted three days. Wasted and weary, I decided enough was enough and announced I was headed home. Needless to say, I should not have been driving! My friend asked innocently enough if I could deliver a package for him to a mutual acquaintance as he handed me a gym bag. On my way home, windows down and music blaring, I ran a stop sign in front of a parked police car.

To make a long story short, he pulled behind me, lights flashing, and I instantly gathered myself in hope of convincingly feigning sobriety. Instead of stopping, I gestured to the officer in my mirror, mockingly knuckling my head, symbolizing that I made a stupid mistake. The officer hit the siren and pulled up to my driver's side window, gesturing for me to pull over. Again, I did the knuckle head routine with a big grin on my face. As dumb luck would have it, the officer recognized me from playing together in a basketball league. He rolled down his window, looked at my eyes, and said, "Hey, Frank, what's up? Have we been partying?" I smiled sheepishly, and he said, "Follow me, I'll get you to your house."

Upon doing my best to drive a straight line, I successfully followed my private escort to the house. I got out of the car and offered the officer my keys. He told me to just get inside and not let him catch my ass out on the street. Without thinking, I grabbed the gym bag out of trunk and walked inside as he watched, then drove away. I snuck in quietly so as not to awaken my mother and locked myself in my room. I sat on my bed and exhaled, pondering what just had happened. My relief lasted until I decided to look inside the bag. Let's just say the contraband contents and amount were enough to have put me away for hard time, had the cop decided to administer a sobriety test and check out the car. My mamá's prayers and God's grace spared me that night.

As my mind returned to my poolside paradise, I wiped the tears from my face and gave thanks, acknowledging that I am no more deserving than any of the voices represented in these pages. It seems God wanted to bring the point home in the here and now. Looking into the pool, I saw what I thought was a large butterfly struggling to stay afloat. Although the water was a bit frigid for this brown boy, I got in to see if I could rescue my little friend. To my surprise, it was not a butterfly, but a beautiful hummingbird. It was shaking slightly and barely alive as I laid it next to me on a towel in the warm sun. I gently blew on it to help dry its gorgeous feathers as I prayed. I must have looked like a crazy man to my neighbor as I sat ministering and speaking out loud to the hummingbird as it slowly came back to life. Soon it was fluttering its wings and pecking my fingers as if to thank me.

For a moment, I pondered making the little vato a pet. The notion lasted only a second as it hit me that no living thing, creature or human, belongs in a cage. I decided to nickname it Alcatraz. He must have approved because he climbed onto my open hand. Holding this precious life gently in my grasp, I stood up, opened my hand and set it free. Alcatraz is no longer a prison, having been returned to its original native inhabitants. It is now home to sacred ceremonies as a symbol of sovereignty. In this blessed moment of revelation, I understood that God was telling me that we are all beautiful, loved and worthy of surviving mistakes and making new lives.

The words of Father Greg Boyle of Dolores Mission and Homeboy Industries echoed in my ear: "If we are all God's children, and God is first and foremost love, then we are created to be the beauty of love incarnate. We are all worthy of love and forgiveness; in fact, forgiveness may be one of the greatest expressions of love." It is through truth in actions, words, songs, danza, prayers and ceremony that we seek,

express and give meaning to this beauty. Yet, the hummingbird, or colibrí, manifests beauty through spirit, sight and simply being. Father Greg, above, is speaking of those he minis-
ters to and loves through the work of Homeboy Industries.
While the men have breached laws and trespassed against others, mistakes for which there may be consequences and lifetime atonement, they are still worthy of love and forgiveness.

The yellow journalism and expediently driven political
hyperbole has scared the public into buying the Super-Predator myth, which has demonized boys and young men of color.
What has resulted is a dehumanization and malign neglect
that places this part of the American family in peril. Very little has been done to improve their life chances out of poverty.
Over six million Latino children still live in poverty. Sixty
years after *Brown v Board of Education*, 50 percent of Latino,
Black, and Native youth still drop out before completing high
school. Zero tolerance, suspension and expulsion policies have
legally removed our children from public schools and pushed
them out onto the streets. Between 1972 and 2014, the
national prison population has increased from 300,000 to 2.3
million (Jobs Not Jails, 2014). The population of juvenile
detention centers, prisons and other correctional institutional
structures directly mirrors the school dropout demographic.

Our purpose for presenting this book *Latino Young Men and
Boys in Search of Justice: Testimonies*, is to lift up expressions by
Latinos through poetry, writings and arte that capture and
appeal to the common humanity shared by us all. These are
people lifting up their experiences, brokenness, remorse,
lamentations and hopes for atonement, forgiveness, redemption and rebirth. We also offer the voice of leaders and community advocates seeking to change the circumstances that
poverty, discrimination and inequality creates; the intent is to
help heal wounded individuals, families and communities; and

mend the broken relations in our society. A key front of this social reform is the adoption of the values and strategies of Restorative or Transformative Justice. The featured writings in this book seek to harness a chorus of voices to articulate and promote a more humane, comprehensive public sector and a community-based response to crime, punishment, rehabilitation, healing, reconciliation and restorative value-based strategies in the administration of justice and the corrections system. These include especially collective efforts supporting the successful return of Latino boys and young men to their families, community and society, i.e., comprehensive re-entry.

As human beings, we are capable of higher expression of love and hate, beauty and pain, rhapsody and suffering, truth and revelation; we are also capable of trespass and violence, remorse and atonement, forgiveness and redemption. We offer these expressions of truth, pain and beauty through words and art, in hopes of opening your hearts and minds to new ways of realizing justice and democracy in America. When we love or are manifesting our creative spirit, we are living in the heart of God.

Tomás Alejo, tattoo artist and activist

Hummingbird Spirit

A hummingbird as an apparition
Of life in perfection
Duality of substance and spirit
Hovering among us in absolute beauty
Try though we may to behold
Its feathered tapestry of colors
The nuanced touch of a Divine hand
Its making is beyond the pale of sight
Gentle eyes a window
To the infinite bounds of love
As it darts outside our focus
The hummingbird breathes
Only to taste the nectar of creation
In the subtle song of its wings
Is the harmony of prayer
Touching the distal corners of time
A wordless prophesy
The absolute beauty in all of us
Forging one circle of accord
See the hummingbird in you
Bleeding in and out of presence
Yet constant on the mind
Effortlessly spreading the sweetness
Of the nectar that all should taste
A wisdom that heals
Heart to heart and place to place
Gathering pain and prayers
Sprouting seeds of hope
Healing touch of forgiveness

Blessing us ever so gently
With the quiet song of its wings
A glimpse of infinite beauty, love
A gentle kiss from God.

Essays, Poems and Reflective Writings from Intergenerational Voices

The essays presented in this section are intended to provide an authoritative introduction to the La Cultura Cura philosophy and framework, as well as an overview of guiding values and policy concepts for adopting a restorative juvenile and criminal justice system and insights into two leading models of restorative justice and community change.

The Legacy of Cultural Arts and Activism

Richard Montoya

The impact of teatro, artists and poets like my father, José Montoya, is intimately interwoven in virtually every front of Chicano Movement history. As a playwright and filmmaker, I came out of the 1980s when there was a truly thriving Chicano Teatro; at one point in California there were some 70 active teatro groups. It was like each barrio had its own troupe. This was really the outgrowth of the 1960s and 1970s Movimiento, which gave rise to teatro and the cultural arts as a potent tool. Artists, muralists, poets and musicians such as my dad had become part of the movement's communal voice, conscience and memory. There was an explosion of teatro that had come in waves, such as El Teatro Campesino's *"El Fin del Mundo,"* with part one, two, five, giving rise to the monumental phenomenon that was "Zoot Suit." Mundo was always the homeboy. *El pachuco, y el vato loco del barrio.*

By the time we formed Culture Clash in 1984 (Ric Salinas, Herbert Sigüenza and me), a lot of these troupes were gone. Nevertheless, such groups as El Teatro Campesino, El Teatro de la Esperanza, Teatro Denver and maybe ten other groups stayed vibrant. Collectively, these artists planted the flag: the performing arts, music and poetry became the voice of authentic Chicano, Latino, Indígena experience and identity, preserving history, tradition, expression and celebration rooted in cultura. These many expressions through teatro, music, poet-

3

ry, artwork and murals were brilliant portrayals, sharp as a blade. It was us, by us, for us. It was our sharing with the world of our beauty and sacredness as people.

I was exposed through my father and his lifetime of work. His involvement in the struggle included joining César Chávez in the fields. In 1969, my dad and his colleagues Esteban Villa, Juanishi V. Orosco, Ricardo Favela and Rudy Cuéllar were teaching art in Sacramento. Frustrated with the marginalization of Chicano artists, they formed an art collective that blossomed into a movement to support the budding farm workers' union. These artists produced many of the iconic art, posters and images associated even today with the UFW, including the famous "HUELGA" eagle flag. The collective named itself the Royal Chicano Air Force (RCAF). I am proud of the historical legacy of my father, to be counted among his contemporary cultural warriors: Malaquías Montoya, Rodolfo "Corky" Gonzales, Lalo Guerrero, Guillermo Gómez Peña, Ester Hernández, and Luis Valdez.

So many amazing men and women who used the broad realm of cultural arts as an instrument of education, advocacy, organizing and building community agency to support change in the human condition. Cultura and arte became points of authority for the Movimiento, proclaiming our sovereignty, preserving our true history, expressing our diverse identity and realizing justice. I remember one time my father leaving the house at 3 am with fellow members of the RCAF. They had designed a giant thematic mural for unveiling at a September 16th rally outside of Folsom Prison. They wanted their incarcerated brothers (as well as the prison authorities) to wake up and see they were remembered and supported in their right to hold ceremony and sweat-lodge while incarcerated.

Arte is also a medicine for our community, particularly the healing of young ones, their restorative education, character, social and political development. In my early work with Teatro de la Calle and later with Culture Clash we carried on these activist arte traditions of performing in the fields, on the streets, in schools, colleges churches, and prisons—wherever the message took us. Arte is a powerful non-violent weapon capable of transforming hearts and minds. Even when shared in the "mainstream," political satire, poetry, song, filmmaking and the various expressions of the arts deliver painful truths about social ills told in a palatable yet honestly incisive communique. Culture Clash plays have always tried to honor arte as a catalyst force, taking on such issues as the unhealed wounds of conquest, racism, corporate greed, police abuse, immigration policy, hypocrisy, political corruption, worker rights and gentrification.

In a screenplay I wrote that was just released in a full-length Indie Film, tell a story of *real politique*, power, culture and the often unseen face of Los Angeles when told through Latino eyes and experience. Presently, Culture Clash is performing a revival of its play, "Chavez Ravine"—an original and true story evoking the dark American legacy of Manifest Destiny. The play is the account of modern-day annexation of land, destruction of community and forced uprooting of poor people of color in the "building" of Los Angeles. An original gentrification L.A. story!

Under the arbitrary powers of imminent domain, three beautiful barrios were forcibly taken away from poor people of color, ostensibly to make room for a large public housing project. After the land lay dormant for 10 years, the land was sold to make way for what is now Dodger Stadium. It was a dark time in Los Angeles history. As social anthropologists, Culture Clash seeks to unearth those untold stories and history of multicultural communities that are otherwise erased or ignored. Painful human experiences poetically, spiritually and satirically presented in the spirit of truth and reconciliation, they are America's historical anathemas told in a good way. The goal of the play was not to stage a comprehensive critical history, but to open hearts, evoke conscience and provide an altar to find mutual understanding of honest history.

There are so many challenges facing our communities, inter-generational trauma from poverty and injustice, forces of division, and miseducation; we use our art form to fight back. This is what I was taught and witnessed as the son of a cultural warrior and now as a culture warrior in my own right. I appreciate the groups and organizations that embrace the arts as a strategy of La Cultura Cura. Such groups as Barrios Unidos, Tía Chucha's Cultural Center, Corazón del Pueblo, Self-Help Graphics, the Compadres Network Círculos, Homeboys Industries, Homies Unidos and other art programs, traditional or contemporary music, hip hop, spoken word, drum circles, ceremonies and danza troupes that have taken root in the community. Danza troupes like Izcalli have grown right out of this cultural renaissance.

That is what I appreciate the most about my father's and his contemporary cultural warriors, their art, poetry, music, teatro and writings hinged on organic connection to the heartbeat of the people, the authentic representation of their experiences and hopes. Through the arts they humanized those people who were demonized or discarded by the dominant culture the most: immigrants, pachucos, homeboys, farm workers, laborers, prisoners, our objectified women and vilified young ones. They portrayed the beauty of the least powerful, capturing their sacredness, dignity and their humble elegance. The power of movement art is that it lifts up the true beauty of our cultura, our truth, our place in the human family, la causa. It creates a collective consciousness, inter-connectedness, a pathway to explore the origins and evolution of our diverse, authentic identity and purpose as la raza cósmica.

In my father's passing, he wrote a final three books with his last breaths—three long poetic breaths to last a lifetime. A breath: like a poem or a book of humility. Another breath: a book of courage. The final breath: a book of surrender and dig-nity. He taught me by his life example that it is in our being genuinely Chicano, Latino and Indio that we manifest our true gifts for the world. He was a true multiculturalist. Our cul-ture is the river tributary that carries us to join that place of universal humanity. We need to encourage this sentimiento or world view in our young and emerging poets, writers, artists, musicians, storytellers and social advocates. I hope that the people who read this book, those who breathe in its poems, writings and art, are moved to see their own sacredness and connectedness in the lives of those this society has discarded, removed and locked away in prisons from family, community and society. A collective spirit, heart and voice calls out to us from these pages.

The Moral Imperative of Restorative and Transformative Justice

Javier Stauring

Restorative justice seeks to balance justice and mercy. The goal of restorative justice is to heal, reconcile and restore both victim and offender. We define the victim to include the individuals involved, families, communities and society. Of course, we must reach and transform policy, the justice system, law enforcement and systems officials to truly affect change; balance responsibility and restitution that restores dignity, purpose and balance to the whole. The dignity of each person is the foundation of the moral vision of society; we are all sacred.

In Catholic teachings, we try to balance responsibility and restitution that restores dignity, purpose and balance to the whole. All people are not only social but also sacred. How we organize our society, including law and policy, directly affects human dignity and the capacity of individuals to grow in community.

Punishment and the power to suspend rights and freedoms are to be wielded with compassionate discretion; all in order to defend the public order, advance the common good and restore harmony in social relationships. Our Catholic tradition leads us to try to balance justice and mercy in dealing with those who break society's laws. For us, punishment must be more than making criminals "pay" for their crimes. Punishment should protect society, defend the public order and restore harmony in the social relationships disrupted by crimes.

But our punishments must also be "medicinal." Our punishments must contribute to the moral correction and education of criminals. We must seek to "restore" them as productive members of society. Our archdiocesan Office of Restorative Justice oversees many projects that reflect this Catholic understanding of crime and punishment. Our Catholic tradition leads us to try to balance justice and mercy in dealing with those who break society's laws. For us, punishment must be more than making criminals "pay" for their crimes.

The following letter to the church written by Catholic Archbishop José H. Gómez, captures a beautiful summation of Christian principles regarding justice in matters of crime and punishment:

> . . . We provide chaplains to the many correctional facilities located within the Archdiocese. We offer spiritual support and healing for crime victims and their families. We minister to men and women in jail. We offer spiritual assistance to their families—especially to the many children who have parents who are in prison. This work of "restorative justice" is vital to the Church's mission of creating a city of love and truth and a culture of peace and reconciliation. It's not easy to love those who commit violence and other crimes. . . . This doesn't mean that we forget their crimes—or their victims. It does mean that we treat criminals with dignity and respect their rights. Loving the guilty means we can never give up on them. We need to always be seeking the conversion and repentance of criminals and those already behind bars. We need to get these people to take responsibility for their

actions and to make restitution. But we also need to get them to change their lives—so they can live with the dignity and purpose for which God made them. So let's work to build a culture where our justice is always tempered by our mercy—and by our hope for the redemption of sinners. And let's pray in a very special way for the victims of violent crimes and their families, so that through the healing grace of God, they may have the strength to endure their pain, and at the same time, find forgiveness and peace of heart.

Lifting Latinos Up by their Rootstraps: Moving Beyond Trauma Through a Healing-Informed Framework for Latino Boys and Men

Frank de Jesús Acosta and Jerry Tello

The 16 million Chicano/Latino children and youth currently in America represent a crucial segment of our country's future workers, taxpayers, parents, citizens, voters and leaders (National Council of La Raza, 2010). More than one Latino child in three (35%) is poor, compared to one white child in eight, making them less likely to finish high school, more likely to be poor as young adults and less likely to be working between the ages of 25 and 29. That Latino teens are currently more than twice as likely as other youth to drop out of high school (Chapman et al., 2010), coupled with the many additional risks these young people face from exposure to protracted poverty, should concern all Americans.

Ever-larger shares of Latino children are facing a decade of crisis in America (Snyder and Dillow, 2011). Currently, Latinos make up the majority population in juvenile detention centers and juveniles in prison. Despite the profound health, educational and socio-economic inequities facing Latinos, targeting funding and culturally relevant programming for this significant population is sparse and is failing to meet its unique needs. Furthermore, any innovation in addressing these disparities requires investments that move away from "trauma-informed care" and generic wraparound service systems. In its

11

place would be a "healing-informed," culturally specific approach for service delivery that is rooted in long-overlooked indigenous principles and practices, as well as funding that focuses specifically on the needs of Latino boys and men.

Leading philanthropic organizations, such as The California Endowment, Ford Foundation, Robert Wood Johnson Foundation, W. K. Kellogg Foundation, California Community Foundation, Sierra Health Foundation and Liberty Hill Foundation have sounded the clarion call on the crisis state in the welfare of boys and men of color across the nation. Nationally, the demographics of our population are changing at an accelerated pace. According to the Urban Institute, ethnic minorities now make up 46 percent of all children. By 2023, the majority of children will be people of color. The number of Latino children under the age of 18 living in the United States has doubled in the last two decades, making Latinos one of the fastest growing segments of the national population. By 2035, one-third of all American children will be of Latino descent.

Today, there are over 16 million Chicano/Latino children and youth—92 percent of whom are U.S. citizens—who represent a crucial segment of our country's future workforce, taxpayers, parents, citizens, voters and leaders (National Council of La Raza, 2010). Despite these clear demographic trajectories, resources to address the health and socio-economic disparities Latinos face in daily life are sparse. In fact, support through targeted funding towards building culturally relevant programming to better serve the Latino populace has been minimal. To address these disparities, this essay will serve to elucidate a process for moving trauma-informed care and service systems to a culturally specific, healing-informed model for service delivery. Specifically, in this way we encourage the provision of funds and resources to provide more focused and responsive attention on the needs of Latino and Native boys and young men.

We are not speaking in isolation about the need for a more culturally relevant, healing-informed approach. A substantive body of literature exploring health and socio-economic disparities, disproportional exposure to violence and the resultant trauma facing boys and young men of color is rapidly amassing (John Rich, et al. "Healing the Hurt: Trauma-Informed Approaches to the Health of Boys and Young Men of Color." Drexel University School of Public Health: Center for Nonviolence and Social Justice and Drexel University College of Medicine, Department of Emergency Medicine, 2009; Lois Davis, et al, "Reparable Harm: Assessing and Addressing Disparities Faced by Boys and Men of Color in California," Rand Corporation, 2009.) These research efforts have served to legitimize Boys and Men of Color (BMoC) as a field of inquiry, greatly advancing contemporary thinking and universal responses that surround this population. Additionally, the BMoC field has identified gaps of knowledge and informed the field on the causes of and solutions to disparity and disparity-induced trauma.

Despite these efforts, the reality is that the majority of these investigations and program development frameworks have focused most intensively on African Americans, thus marginalizing the specific culturally based needs of Chicano/Latino and Native populations. Clearly, the needs of African Americans are significant and pressing. They deserve on-going intensive attention; but, plainly stated, there are essential knowledge and funding gaps in the present body of work that do not address the experiences of other needy populations of boys and young men that reside in communities throughout the United States, specifically Chicano/Latino and Native boys and men.

Foundational to the concepts presented in the full version of this essay is a better understanding of who Latinos are as a people and diverse culture. The "Latino" identity in American mainstream society is often viewed as monolithic. In fact, the term Latino casts a wide net often based solely on language, when in fact it includes people from many countries, cultural traditions, mixed ancestry, histories, with some similarities and significant important distinctions.

For instance, in California and the Southwest, Chicano/ Latino populations include a majority of persons with indigenous ancestral cultural roots tied both to Mexico and Central America. In California, the east coast and throughout the country there are equally significant representations of Latinos from South America, Puerto Rico, the Dominican Republic and Cuba with ancestral mixes that include indigenous, African and Asian roots. All have their own culture, spirituality and authentic selves, which face healing and recovery from the disequilibrium of forced western assimilation and acculturation. Race matters, but it is culture and its associated values, virtues and traditions that truly define a person and a group's identity; and that most often determine their well-being as individuals, families, communities and members of a pluralistic society.

Culturally relevant innovation and capacity currently exist, but require replication in order to fully inform the prevention field of the disparity impacting Latino and Native boys and men. At the programmatic level, La Cultura Cura, or Culture-Based Healing, is a method for healing and healthy development which is inextricably linked to restoring one's true cultural identity as the foundation of well-being for individuals, families, communities and society alike. It employs a multigenerational process of learning and/or remembering one's true and positive cultural values, principles, customs and traditions. To promulgate La Cultura Cura at the systems and institutional levels, the National Compadres Network, which has been a leader in the field, will expand the group's innovative, healing-informed program, known as La Cultura Cura

Healing Generations. This effort provides a framework and process to transform the experiences of Latino and Native men and boys, their families and communities beyond the current model of identifying trauma, instead moving toward a prosperous and thriving community. This will be accomplished through:

- Culturally rooted and responsive programming
- Provider network and capacity-building
- Transformation of systems from trauma- to healing-informed efforts

La Cultura Cura Healing Generations is a self-sustaining framework that taps into a resource-rich cadre of experts and elders who can transform the national dialog, inform policy and enrich community capacity. It aims to be part of the efforts to address longstanding issues through a culturally framed, asset-based approach. La Cultural Cura Healing Generations integrates this healing-informed approach into education, engagement, delivery of prevention and/or intervention services and service aftercare as a vital first step in reducing life-threatening outcomes for Latino and Native boys and men.

Through La Cultura Cura Healing Generations, funders, practitioners and the communities impacted by historical racial oppression possess a framework to translate culturally grounded tenets into systems transformation. To bring this framework to scale, a comprehensive approach is necessary that includes policy and systems change, best achieved through the following recommended actions:

1. Increase programmatic support for integrating a healing-informed framework that focuses on fostering natural opportunity factors and building resilience.
2. Develop pathways to health and well-being for Latino and Native males through culturally grounded and responsive physical, emotional, mental and spiritual development.
3. Support community-acknowledged Latino and indigenous organizations to develop and evaluate best practices, comprehensive community strategies and program models that directly address what we call "Chronic Traumatic Stress Disorder" (CTSD), while encircling the individual, families and entire community in healing, restorative and development processes.
4. Train personnel working all levels of educational, criminal justice, mental health, health and social services in the culturally based, healing-informed approach for serving Latino and Native men and boys, so those systems can recognize and adapt their efforts to be more responsive to the Latino and Native males they are charged to serve.
5. Support programs that promote the involvement of Latino and Native mothers and fathers in the schools. Education is the foundation for economic mobility in the United States, as well as an important and healthy pathway for the integration of immigrants into society.
6. Support the development of generational extended-kinship networks and "Círculo" healing support groups to provide positive indigenous male support for young men in all communities.
7. Inform mental health and social service providers, including practitioners, supervisors, agencies and funding sources, of the benefits of using this framework to

better serve the needs of their clientele, by utilizing cultural assets that Latino and Native families and communities possess.

Systems Recommendations:

1. Acknowledge within the Boys and Men of Color (BMoC) field that, for Latino and Native males, the path to healing and healthy development is inextricably linked to restoring one's true cultural identity and recognizing the origins of unhealthy and maladapted behaviors.
2. Shift the BMoC field from the present deficit-based paradigm that is dominant in the field to one that is healing-informed, through strategies that place the individual, family and community as the priority in the implementation of healing and restorative strategies.
3. Promote intercultural exchange and learning across the BMoC field to establish culturally based best practices that foster comprehensive responses and/or frameworks, while recognizing the legitimacy of diverse tenets of culture, distinct experiences and world perspectives of different racial and cultural groups.
4. Review and reinforce the development of cultural-proficiency standards that lead to practices and professional standards and policies in service delivery systems that reach and engage Latino and Native boys and men. The goal of this effort is to identify and eliminate discriminatory standards that impede the serving of vulnerable groups in education, shelters, hospitals and clinics, and other similar settings.
5. Move the social services and helping field to understand that developing cultural proficiency in any profession requires ongoing education and introspection in order

to fully address the power imbalance between providers and the populations they serve. Additionally, introduce the concept of "cultural humility" as a way for providers to better serve Latino and Native males (Tervalon and Murray-Garcia, 1998).

6. Prioritize policy and systems change that improves cultural humility in K-12 education.

Funder Recommendations:

1. Target public and private funds for investigation, research and demonstration directed at unearthing the unique needs and cultural capital of Latino and Native males.
2. Increase public and private investment support for schools and other community-based educational models that teach cultural humility with academic rigor and prepare students for participation in the workforce and vocational training.
3. Increase cross sector support for schools and other community-based strategies promoting the civic and economic advancement of immigrants within the United States.
4. Leverage philanthropic support to cultivate the collective impact that can be achieved through community-based organization partnerships that align comprehensive community-building strategies among public agencies, safety net providers, local schools, adult schools, community colleges, businesses and labor.

Since 2012, the National Compadres Network (NCN) has expanded demonstration of its "Círculo and Cultura Cura Model" locally in California as well as nationally. Many communities addressing boys and young men issues have sought NCN assistance to integrate cultural and spiritual healing into their work, including communities in Denver, San Antonio and

Baltimore. We did this on several fronts including: 1) Informing policy in juvenile justice reform towards what NCN calls "Transformative Justice Strategies"; 2) Institutional trainings and capacity building on culturally based approaches; 3) technical assistance and training to implement the various topical curricula (e.g., Joven Noble/Responsible Manhood); 4) intensive capacity building and service delivery in 14 communities in California.

The NCN, along with several of our organizational allies addressing the crisis facing Chicano/Latino and Indigenous boys and young men, has made tremendous inroads in changing the national narrative beyond the black/white paradigm or black/white binary that dominates policy and philanthropic attention. Just on the basis of history, fairness and proportionality of population, Chicanos/Latinos and Native people must not be excluded from equal consideration. Dialogs and initiatives addressing boys and young men issues increasingly include representation of Chicano/Latino and Native voices in racial justice and racial healing efforts. This includes participation in the White House "My Brothers' Keeper Initiative," established to address the "School to Prison Pipeline," and nascent efforts to redesign and implement reforms to juvenile justice corrections strategies and school achievement disparities. A White House webinar featured NCN multi-topic cultural curricula for a national audience of practitioners, policy makers and stakeholders.

NCN was brought together in a multi-cultural national gathering of "Wisdom Keepers" in February 2015 to further the depth of the work in building culturally competent leaders and trainers from the fields of fatherhood, rites of passage, health, education, family violence, teen pregnancy prevention, transformative juvenile justice, social service, advocacy, trauma healing and evidence-based research. This kind of conference is essential to moving the public narrative and understanding of culturally competent best practices that are multi-culturally inclusive as well as culture specific. The expanded dialog ultimately yields more comprehensive and effective policy and systems change and, hopefully, better informs the alignment and distribution of funding and resources.

These evolving activities are important because they allow us to expand the narrative about who we are as a diverse Raza, establishing the recognition and political agency warranted by our history on this continent and ending the cycle of disparity for our children and the next generation. The Wisdom Keeper gathering stressed primary teachings across cultures, that we are all sacred; this is the essence of Cultura Cura. These efforts must also be inter-generational; inclusive of youth and elders, with meaningful consideration for gay, lesbian, bi-sexual and transgender populations while intimately involving the voice of the woman nation. The inter-connected sacredness of all people is the basis for healing, building community, creating inter-ethic respect and a pluralistic democratic society.

It must be recognized by the field and key stakeholders that approaches targeting Chicano/Latino and Native populations that are not rooted in a cultural framework and healing are not reducing violence, gang involvement, substance abuse, teen pregnancy, or preventing dropping out of school and incarceration recidivism. Universal western institutional approaches often miss the essential ingredient of healing, spirituality and sacredness. The Cultura Cura framework not only solves immediate issues such as violence, but also provides knowledge and capacity within the community to build protective preventive capacities, restores the cultural communal fabric and structures (e.g., community learning, talking, healing, mediation and action circles) while healing, strengthening and enabling people across generations. Healthy individuals, families and communities are those re-rooted in cultural mores, values, traditions, human sacredness, inter-connectedness and purpose. For instance, in Salinas, California, NCN trained 120 people as circle keepers. These people assumed leadership after a rash of shootings threatened community stability. They organized learning and healing circles that staved off more shootings.

A critically important front of our work is knowledge and capacity building within anchor institutions, including schools, justice systems, law enforcement, health, public agencies, safety net provider networks, higher education, businesses and labor institutions. Building a leadership base and critical mass of Cultura Cura-versed practitioners allows for the alignment and complementary impact of community and institutional integrated efforts in addressing and changing the structures and ethos of disparity. Another example is our work with the social justice media and advocacy organization Race Forward. Working within our Cultura Cura Healing Generations training modules and community "Círculos" (or Circles), we have brought together community with police, probation and school officials to advance Racial Justice and Healing Practices addressing the connection between educational system failures, involvement with the justice system, recidivism prevention and re-entry.

The greater integration of community- and institution-based activities will now become a regular element in sites where NCN is building local cultural competency capacity, sustainability, policy and systems change. The Cultura Cura Healing Generations model is being shared as partnerships and funding resources allow in connection with our current alliances involving The California Endowment Building Healthy Communities Initiative, the Alliance for Justice, Gathering for Justice, the White House-sponsored My Brother's Keeper initiative and other efforts like the Wisdom Keeper Gathering. For more information see: www.nationalcompadresnetwork.org and www.nlffi.org.

Restorative Justice: Building Community Agency

George Galvis

Born in the San Francisco Bay Area, I was raised in a single parent household. One of my most vivid childhood memories was being three years old and having to go over to the neighbor's house to call the cops on my father for beating my mom severely. Domestic violence defined our home for a long time until my mother made the difficult choice of leaving my father for good. I still have a visceral recollection of those difficult times, which over time manifested as anger and violence in my own life on the streets.

At seven years of age, I was placed in a gifted education magnet program in the San Francisco school system. Most of the students were from white middle class families that were bused into the school. This exposed me to the whole notion of "American" culture as it was impressed on me daily. I was the low-income kid on government assistance (e.g., Section VIII, AFDC and food stamps) with a single parent domestic violence survivor as head-of-household. My only extended family was my grandma, an uncle with drug-induced mental health issues and an alcoholic grandfather.

At thirteen, I began to recognize my cultural differences and started resisting the Eurocentric values forced on me at school. It became more and more apparent that I was treated differently from my classmates. My first experiences with racism started with being blamed anytime something was stolen or broken or defaced. Teachers and administrators just figured if I didn't do it, I knew who did. Soon, what I now know to be racial profiling started happening to me on the streets. If I wasn't being called into the office at school, I was routinely hassled on the streets by the police for no reason. It only made me angrier and angrier to learn about things like civil, legal and equal rights in the classroom and then have my daily experiences teaching me different.

A poignant life lesson came when I was stopped by police in the aftermath of a big fight that had broken out at school. The police had been called in to control the situation and ended up singling me out for questioning right in front of our school principal. When I spoke up for myself about not having done anything wrong and having rights, the cop straight out punched me in the face. I was shocked to find that the principal, who I looked to protect me, just turned away and said nothing. This was the defining moment when I learned the color of my skin meant not being treated equally or with the same regard as my white "peers."

I began to rebel in school and seek my validation by the rules of the street among people who looked like me. Over time, after some hard knocks, I ascertained the falsehood of the laws of the street and gang culture. For awhile, though, this was my path and vehicle of rebellion, my warped place of belonging. The violence, faux code of honor and manhood, fratricide and madness on the streets became my world of reference until a crossroad just before I turned eighteen. The moment of truth came after several incidents brought me into contact with the juvenile justice system. I was headed nowhere fast!

At seventeen, I found myself facing a case with a significant sentence in the California Youth Authority (CYA). Were it not for my mother's impassioned plea to the juvenile court judge, I would likely have received a sentence that condemned me to a legacy of jails and prisons rather than a chance that saved my life. My mother convinced the judge that I had promise and to allow me to go overseas to study at a military academy in Columbia come the fall school year. As luck would have it, weeks before I was scheduled to leave, the Colombian relatives that were going to host me called to inform my mom that they would not be able to take me in after all. It worked out, however, as the probation officer took it upon himself not to send me back to court for resentencing; instead, he informed my mom that if I stayed in school, got a job and did not get in any trouble with the law, he would not consider me in violation of my probation.

In 1993, with the specter of CYA detention hanging over my head, I began my healing path. I went to work full-time and enrolled in community college in San Mateo. I chose San Mateo to avoid going back to my old neighborhood and old ways. It was here that I met the circle of people who shared my background and experiences with gangs, streets and violence—people also looking to make a change in their lives and in the community. I began volunteering at the Barrio Youth Project with some friends. On one outing we took a group of young people to a community peace conference. This was the first time I met the person who would become my teacher and mentor, renowned community leader Daniel "Nane" Alejandrez, founder of the Santa Cruz Barrios Unidos community peace movement.

Listening as Nane openly talk about his violent past, struggles with addiction and family history of incarceration made me want to know more about his journey of redemption and healing. As he spoke of the Barrios Unidos framework of cultural awareness, education and community involvement to promote justice, peace and real social change, he also created a spiritual environment that moved me and the group. It was exactly this path of healing culture that our young people needed to understand and needed to see. It was the healing culture that changed my life forever and the lives of my friends who also heard Nane speak that day. La Cultura Cura became our guiding philosophy and strategy upon returning to San Mateo. Building locally on this work, we founded the San Mateo chapter of Barrios Unidos.

My own healing and revelation truly took root here; I realized that Nane's story, my story and the experiences of others like us need not be stories of shame, but rather of redemption and promise. There was a sense of authenticity and integrity in involving people who came out of the experiences of violence, gangs and street culture; incorporating the power of their own transformation to support change in others and the community. The cultural dimension of the work is the main ingredient. La Cultura is learning and returning with understanding to live according to the values, principles, virtues, traditions and practices of ones' cultural heritage. These are central to our personal, familial and communal well-being and to realizing our human potential, as well as healthy co-existence with others.

During this time, I was also re-introduced to an elder of the American Indian Movement (AIM) who taught me how to walk the Red Road to recovery and healing, to return to the old ways and virtues of living that keep us whole. These ways of living and being connected to each other, to community, have become the central tenets of how I see restorative justice. For example, in our traditional ways, we incorporate "community circles," not courts, to deal with wrongs or harm to others in the community. These circles serve as safe places where the medicines of ceremony are used to create openness to the sharing of pain mis-steps in our journeys, or related transgressions against one another's well-being. They involve sharing fears, frailties and dreams; finding, giving and forgiveness. Latino men who lose this indigenous way of being do not often find places where they can share with true candor and intimacy. Participation in these "Community Healing Circles" has found a central place in the work I now do at Communities United for Restorative Youth Justice (CURYJ).

My studies at the University of California-Berkeley focused on understanding culturally and spiritually based approaches to healing youth violence and gang intervention. It was there that I deepened my community-based instruction from Sundancer Albino García, the architect of the culturally based curricular framework utilized at Santa Cruz Barrios Unidos. In fact, he served as my thesis advisor and informed my continuing work with the San Mateo Chapter of Barrios Unidos in the East Bay of Oakland. I also met and began to learn from the work of elder Jerry Tello, perhaps the leading thinker in philosophy, theory of change and program design authentically based in La Cultura Cura.

My master's thesis focused on the Barrios Unidos violence prevention model, which is dedicated to healing youth and families, preparing new leaders and advancing the study and application of new methods of peace- and justice-oriented education, organizing, inter-generational civic engagement, youth leadership development, community empowerment and economic empowerment. A particular focus of my studies was the Rites of Passage Framework developed for the Barrios Unidos César Chávez School for Social Change and designed by Albino. The groundbreaking curriculum laid out developmental steps rooted in indigenous values, principles and traditions, from childhood to responsible adulthood. The curriculum incorporated Jerry Tello's recovery and healing teachings as an essential element based on the premise that Latino boys and men carry a genetic memory of oppression from colonization, causing trauma and leaving them in a state of post-colonial stress disorder, which is passed from generation to generation.

The answer for many of us who come from this chain of disparity and brokenness is the healing and wholeness that Cultura brings. For example, a fundamental teaching of Cultura imparted to a young child is "inter-connectedness" and "belonging" to all in the human family—in the Mayan tradition this life tenet is called *"In Lak'ech Hala Ken"* (i.e., I am the other you and you are the other me)—or, "All My Relations" used among northern tribal nations. This becomes the cornerstone of our worldview, our fundamental inter-connectedness and inter-dependence to one another as a human family. We also teach our children and reinforce during their stages of development to responsible adulthood that they all have gifts and a sacred purpose.

What happens in this broken society is that our children grow up without getting their chance to share their gifts or find their sacred purpose. It is simple common sense social math: Children who grow up not getting to feel like they are good for something, or good at something, are going to end up being bad. This is what happened to me. Until I was fortunate to experience the healing path, I became a negative force in the world. What many of us who have espoused the beauty and power of cultura want to do is share it with our lost young ones. To help them heal and become the noble person they were born to be is not an easy proposition in a society where they have been traumatized, demonized, vilified and convicted at birth.

Growing up with people who looked like me (in proximity to those who didn't) and always being the first to be blamed when something went wrong, at school, the park and the streets; always the suspect; deemed guilty whether I committed the wrong or not told me early on in life where my people sit in the social hierarchy; I learned that a profile of negativity was long ago cast and created for us, so it always fits. Anything deemed negative, destructive, violent or criminal was stacked atop the profile—embellished over generations—becoming labels and an ever-present stigma for our young. The predator myth, espoused by conservatives and moderates alike, became the impetus for almost three decades of the most draconian social policy and institutional practice witnessed since legal segregation.

Narrow-sighted racist policy and practice that was punishment based: law enforcement, juvenile and criminal justice, trying and incarcerating children as adults, and a mudslide of repugnantly discriminatory polices targeting schools serving children of color. This has been a period of institutional racism and discrimination at its ugliest heights. Sadly, too many of our young ones succumbed to the stigma, internalizing this oppression that often became a self-fulfilling prophesy. The recalcitrance of this trauma is in addition to the modern stresses imposed on families and communities of color by society. The fact is, when we work with our young ones to undo the harm done by the counter cultures of gangs, street and thug life, we still must deal with the damage done by forceful indoctrination of the one-size-fits-all Anglo-Saxon-Protestant capitalist ethic imposed by colonialism and hegemony.

What happens to indigenous people in a society where our cultures are systematically taken from us through forced acculturation is that we rebel and create counter-cultures such as gangs, pachucos and street culture with their own faux codes, values and principles of survival. These are forged in poverty, inequality, alienation and visceral responses to racism, which in turn breed desperation, anger, violence, nihilism and defiant anti-social behaviors towards those same entities that would treat us this way and control the power to change these circumstances. In these counter cultures, the rites of passage, values of honor, community, loyalty, courage, strength, man-hood (e.g., machismo and misogyny) and womanhood are dis-torted and self-destructive, breaking down our own most resilient familial, communal and social fabric. In many ways, our young come to mimic the worst elements of colonization.

Upon closer examination of counter cultures, such as gangs, we will inevitably find cultural icons, images, spiritual symbols, even hybrid communal values and principles within gang and street cultures. These are expressions of our cultural DNA trying to surface. This can even be applied to tattooing, writing on walls, artwork imagery and rituals—shadows of the ancestral practices that they mimic, resurfacing. These prac-tices tell a story, seeking to resurface history and cultural mem-ory. Unfortunately, these are distortions of culture feeding self-destruction and fratricide, stemming from the wounds of being dehumanized and treated with racial disregard.

In Oakland, 90 percent of the student suspensions and expulsions are for "willful defiance," committed by boys of color. This policy basically means that the schools can suspend students for just about anything. It can be for attire, responding in self-defense, anything teachers want to label as behavioral issues. Such policies do not exist in Bay Area schools with pri-marily white student populations. There are fundamental dif-ferences in school and law enforcement policies and practices based on race, income and geography (e.g., zero tolerance, drug enhancement, gang injunctions and curfews can be found in every school or neighborhood with majority people of color). Disparities of this kind have been increasingly exposed and challenged, creating a window for reform. It starts with acknowledging that the present punitive and punishment-ori-ented approach is discriminatory and has failed miserably.

The political pendulum has moved California increasingly to a window for more creative prevention, intervention and restorative justice-oriented policy and systems change in schools, as well as in the justice and correctional systems. California activists are determined to dismantle and reform the school-to-prison pipeline. Tremendous methodological challenges and opportunities lie ahead in establishing a comprehensive prevention to re-entry model and an aligned institution and community framework. Guiding values must be established to inform the change we need and seek. A period of time will be required to heal the literally thousands of boys and young men already enmeshed in the justice system and its built-in cycles of recidivism to imagine, build and sustain balanced lives.

In January 2011, I became Executive Director of CURYJ. The organization's mission is to interrupt the cycles of violence and poverty by motivating and empowering young people that have been impacted by the criminal justice system. CURYJ believes that youth and young adults are the experts on the issues affecting their lives and need to be involved in developing the policies that impact them. In addition to providing training, technical assistance and organizing support to elevate youth voice and power, CURYJ also creates a place for youth and their families to come together, heal from past experiences, dream and achieve their visions for the future. Towards this end, we provide non-violence and restorative justice training, leadership development, community organizing, legal and policy advocacy, social action research, education, cultural awareness, health and wellness resources.

We are working locally and with advocates across the state to develop a comprehensive support framework and infrastructure that aligns institutional and community resources to provide a pathway for youth and young men to heal and recapture their cultural center by developing knowledge, skills and capacity to advance healthy lives. Generally, in turn, this means returning to family, community and full participation in society—including their return to the Movimiento. Success in community, policy, institutional and social change needs to be inclusive of their voice and agency. An end value of any restorative justice model must be the "wrongdoer's" healing, transformation, engagement and leadership participation in creating a restorative justice paradigm in America as part of their sacred purpose. In this work, participation of all parties, including the victim, is required to restore true balance to community and society. CURYJ enlists the leadership of individuals who have "been through it" across all phases of its work.

We need to eliminate intellectual colonization in our communities. What this means is that external mainstream research has perpetuated the problem by collecting data and stories, and applying their own critical reasoning to better understand and remedy community problems or challenges and then controlling the knowledge as their own. CURYJ conducts its own "Community Participatory Action Research" (CARA) in order to tell our own story and compose an authentic community narrative. CURYJ engages young people and community in conducting their own critical learning and discovery processes to tell their own stories and to define new organic pathways to change and wholeness. This cultural approach is our praxis for individual and community transformation.

Our model of community learning circles follows this approach. For example, in restorative justice circles, youth and community gather to heal, discuss, exchange and reflect on community matters, creating engagement, intimacy and interconnectedness. The process helps facilitate healing, validation, growth, direction, participation and movement for the entire community. The stories and lessons are shared and lifted up in ceremony, promoting integrity, authenticity, ownership and collectiveness in relation to defined strategies for change. This process is not only utilized for advancing justice, dispute resolution, prevention, intervention, re-entry and youth policy, but also to promote needed change on broad issues of community development and well-being.

It will be impossible to create and implement a holistic restorative justice infrastructure without a major cultural shift that moves away from punitive punishment as the cornerstone of the corrective justice process. Building community agency centers on building up people in leadership. Presently, CURYJ works in broad partnerships of community and key institutions to promote the necessary cultural shift. In fact, the culture shift being created with our learning and healing circles is laying the groundwork for essential communal structures that will undergird the capacity for a comprehensive restorative justice infrastructure. A growing number of at-risk youth, ex-offenders and former gang members are being healed, trained and prepared to walk in accountability and responsibility within the community.

Community circles are the vehicle through which CURYJ is building and restoring relationships, both familial and communal, to reintroduce our people to a more traditional and sustaining social fabric with organized structure. Circles are built up within and across neighborhoods and communities, all guided by indigenous cultural values and a growing interconnectedness and shared accountability. Different circles take on different community foci: peace-making circles, school circles, jóvenes (youth) circles, men's circles and women's circles, to name a few. The circles are creating community cohesion, trust, respect and organic moral authority that make a restorative justice paradigm possible. Every circle has its purpose; therefore, each is knowledge based, and communal learning and memory are connected to both a particular and a more collective way of life.

Nascent restorative justice circles include community, the parties involved, a facilitator and institutional players as appropriate (e.g., schools, cops, court officials, probation, safety net providers and community-based organizations). Culture shift at the institutional level is incremental, school by school, court by court, precinct by precinct, through engagement and growing trust. Local community circles already work to resolve "cases" where there was wrong-doing and victimization. The goal of such processes is not only to establish accountability of the person that committed the wrong to another, or that violated a law, in order to levy punishment; rather, the goal is to move all parties towards healing, reconciliation and collective agreement on a corrective path to restore respect and harmony to the community. Without meaningful institutional participation and buy-in, there will be no true change. When the focus is healing, corrective action and respectful, meaningful engagement towards a restorative goal, the results have been amazing.

For instances of minor offences, parole violations and other petty crimes, the case is remanded to a community circle where corrective action, such as school attendance and performance, restitution tasks, community service or counseling, may be the community-monitored remedy. Instead of incarceration, the young person and their family are surrounded by aligned resources along with community accountability and support. It is important to understand that what I am describing here is change from within communities, where a critical mass of people are knowledgeable and committed to bringing institutions along. Deeply rooted change and building of community agency begins informally and organically. Effective communities become models from which others can learn.

We at CURYJ hope you are moved by the heart and spirit of the poetry, writings, art and mural work contributed by our relations in this volume; all of it was created to restore our young ones and families, and to build a healthy vibrant community.

Santa Cruz Barrios Unidos and Restorative Justice

Daniel "Nane" Alejandrez

The Barrios Unidos movement and organization has been at the forefront of providing support, education and advocacy for incarcerated boys and men since it was formed. While this work has taken many forms over the past thirty years, the Santa Cruz Barrios Unidos national chapter has had a steady presence in juvenile detention centers and adult correctional facilities in its surrounding communities and in various sites in the state of California. Our tenets for this work have always been rooted in cultural, spiritual and restorative justice principles (even if they were not always identified by that tag name). We have also been a leading voice in juvenile detention and adult prison reform alliances and in allied local and statewide policy advocacy. Presently, we have innovative culturally based programs operating in local juvenile halls and three adult facilities, as well as parallel on-site community-based programs.

The Juvenile Justice Program

The juvenile hall and juvenile justice activities have been front and center over the past two years with shifting public sentiment providing the first window in thirty years for promoting restorative justice-oriented reform. The California legislature has shown a willingness to completely dismantle the

34

juvenile detention systems as they stand, making it incumbent on the advocacy communities, especially community-based groups like Barrios Unidos, to step up their engagement to work with other advocates, community leadership, policy makers and justice system institutional players to collaborate in building a much more humane and corrective restorative model.

Barrios Unidos works in juvenile halls and detention facilities providing culturally based education, spiritual ceremony and healing, academic support and diverse skill-building activities to help incarcerated boys and young men prepare for their eventual release and build resilience against recidivism. The goal is to use our cultural curricula to restore life affirming values, traditions and positive self-identity. Participants set personal corrective, restorative, developmental and educational goals for their incarceration term as well as for their transition back into family and community life. Barrios Unidos also provides continuous guidance and supports boys, young men and their families, facilitating access to needed support services, counseling, educational resources and safety net services while providing opportunities for positive community engagement.

The Juvenile Evening Reporting Center

The Juvenile Evening Reporting Center is operated at Barrios Unidos in partnership with the Probation Department. The center provides a three-step program along with other support services to assist in meeting conditions of the court and probation. The program involves: 1) cultural identity, spiritual healing and ceremony; 2) motivational and behavioral learning activities; and 3) basic education and skill-building modules. The young men are given access to the Prison Project, a coalition of groups, individuals, community-based organizations and service providers who are dedicated to providing programming, support and hope to prisoners. Since 1994, we have worked with prisoners in institutions across the country as part of a national correspondence program. We have also worked directly within California state prisons, including Deuel Vocational Institute (DVI) in Tracy and Soledad Prison.

The Prison Project

The goal of the Prison Project is to transform the most impoverished and disenfranchised sectors of society: our incarcerated sisters and brothers. This target population is plagued by poverty, violence and abuse. The work of the Prison Project draws from and expands upon the multiple strategies and activities that have been developed over the years by Barrios Unidos staff, which are guided by cultural, spiritual and non-violent principles to promote social justice, economic equity, civic leadership, democratic participation, community development, self-reliance and peace.

The objective of the Prison Project is to bring hope into the lives of incarcerated individuals and to equip them with the tools that will assist them in navigating a constructive developmental path within the institution and ultimately within their own communities. We have seen those involved in the Prison Project remove themselves from being involved in violence and other destructive activities within the institution. Our goal is always to help them achieve parole and ultimately drastically reduce recidivism rates. Many of our program participants have managed to fulfill their parole requirements, reunite with families, maintain their jobs and follow their plan for transitioning back into their respective communities.

By first strengthening and building upon the important and central role of the family, the program seeks to contribute to the cultivation and stabilization of a communal environment within the prison walls. Reintroducing and recapturing cultural and spiritual traditions involves a clear and direct approach of teaching understanding and respect for the dignity of all cultures and spiritual traditions. We help participants harness the power of culture and spirituality to reclaim and restore their lives, prevent future interpersonal violence, avoid re-engagement in gang involvement on their new path to becoming healthy, well-adapted and thriving individuals.

Barrios Unidos also conducts services at the County Jail and on-site under the AB 109 Program providing culturally based and motivational enhancement for pro-social decision making within a life course framework of gang violence and desistance. This includes: 1) enabling their long-term community relationship-building and support with gang members and their families; 2) development of pro-social supports and relationships to replace violent (and related) behavior; 3) providing opportunities to make meaningful contributions through volunteer work tailored to individual skills and interests; 4) providing a consistent social learning environment that teaches and reinforces key concepts of decision-making, alternatives to violence, personal responsibility and pro-social coping skills; 5) on-going mentoring by positive role models who have changed their lives in a positive way; and 6) legal and political advocacy to remove systematic barriers to pro-social involvement and gang desistance.

In fact, in April 2015, Barrios Unidos convened a regional summit, "The State of Latinos in Detention and Incarceration," in Santa Cruz, California. The summit brought together policy experts, foundations, community service providers and practitioners, wardens and probation chiefs. The summit focused on the status and experiences of Latino boys and adults in the state, explored culturally and spiritually based restorative treatment models and engaged participants in critical dialogue on restorative justice policy and systems reform options for juvenile and adult incarceration, corrections and drug treatment strategies. The overriding goal was to create greater understanding and consensus on promising approaches to address the crisis.

Also, in keeping with our fundamental tenet of utilizing culture and art as medicine for those we serve and those we seek to create knowledge-based solidarity in common humanity, Barrios Unidos recently co-sponsored an art exhibition with the William James Association at the Museum of Art & History, featuring Prison Art. The theme, "The Cell and the Sanctuary," featured paintings, drawings and writings by incarcerated individuals in California. Much like the intent of this book, the art and writings sought to capture the first voice experiences, perspectives and humanity of those this nation so willingly discards and warehouses. If prisons are supposed to be about social accountability, we must move beyond punishment to healing and reconciliation among people and between people and society. Art is medicine and a vehicle for such healing, inter-cultural expression and learning, creating new human connection; the power of spirit-driven pencil and paint brush upon a canvas—in this case, our hearts and minds.

Barrios Unidos has assimilated into all areas of its work the connection between cultural consciousness and political action, a commitment to working in inter-racial alliances and coalitions, promoting community self-reliance, economic development and non-violent action for social change. Barrios Unidos is not a traditional youth service organization, but is instead a hybrid social enterprise that works in a holistic fashion with youth, families, the public and the private sectors to build human and community capital, thereby strengthening communities and, as a result, a greater society.

Selected Poems

The ancient practice of poetry, "Flor y Canto," spoken word, storytelling and creative reflective writing, is deeply rooted in pan-Latino-Indio cultural and spiritual traditions. Poetry, writing and spoken creative expression preserve, uncover and move us toward new understandings of a people's life-enhancing cultural values, worldviews and human insights.

The poems and reflective writings featured in this publication were collected through cooperative efforts of our organizational partners, and especially: Communities United for Restorative Youth Justice (CURYJ), Santa Cruz Barrios Unidos, Inside Out Writers and Homies Unidos.

Womb of Culture

Frank de Jesús Acosta

We venerate culture as our worldly womb
Flor y canto, arte essential as a mother's milk
Elemental as air, water and fruits of creation
Culture is lifeblood to our mind and well-being
The spirit fire of love manifests in our heart
Do not deny our tenets of life or native tongue
Or impose yours as indoctrination or hegemony
From dominance we will live in rebellion and dissent
Offer instead, culture songs as a sacred gift, as we do

Poems are the language of our prayers, songs and story
As a road of understanding into the hoop of nations
These are the true ways of respect and agreement
Within each culture resides the beauty of humanity
History, tradition, ingenuity, purpose in our world
Insights Creator gave our ancestors to dwell in harmony
Values and virtues for living in civility, balance, ecology
Culture is our inalienable sacred birthright
Bestowing integrity transcending laws or tyranny

Cultura, the first garments of truth and justice on our nakedness
It is both the flame of imagination and compassion
We are all born in a sovereign womb of culture
From which flow expressions of relation to Earth Mother
Our faith traditions, customs, ceremonies, rites of passage
The adornments of body, home, art, music, literature, faith
These are roots, branches and fruit of the Living Tree
Nourishing and guiding our path to highest human expression
These are our most sacred bond with Creator, humanity,
    creation

Some Advice to Those Who Will Facilitate Arts on the Inside

Freddie Gutiérrez

Writer and Teaching Artist

Communities United for Restorative Youth Justice (CURYJ)

If instead of landing that ideal gig
  at the university
  or the live/work space with studio, stag or gallery
you find yourself volunteering
with people you ain't never known
whose lives you may have only seen at the margins
do say that it is a big thing,
it's like the blossoming of a gnarly tree in winter to the
  person inside.

Do tell the people on the inside
about your life, your struggle
as an artist trying to make ends meet
   trying to forge your artistry with social responsibility
about the margins you write, paint and perform
your way out of.

You may not always understand
a point of view
or bit of prison politics
but remember,
don't trip about the difference
for inside you'll find fields of flowers
   every incarcerated person has a bit of soil to nourish,
think about the seeds and tools that art can offer.

Listen to the nuance of a gesture
catch the shine in one's eyes
when something you present
resonates in the soul
and the group clicks
and you experience a moment of solidarity.

But don't ask for personal revelations on the first day, first
    month even
        the work behind the walls takes time
        remember how long it took for you just to get in
        how long a person locked up has been waiting
        bear in mind the weight of a sentence.

And if the men and woman you learn with
get transferred, put in the hole or released
keep the memory of them alive
in the space between the fire in your chest
and the light within your skull
for they are people,
        much even like you,
                sucker-punched by circumstance
                searching for the viability of their craft
                and shining
                in the dimmest of places.

My People

Ramón Escobar
Inside Out Writers

In our lives we were put in a place in which we did not
    intend to live,
And a place that brain washed us to fail and commit nothing
    but sin.

We grew up to be people that are ignorant and that were
    taught to make bad choices,
That when positive was available and angels came to help
    we ignored their voices.

We grew up in a world that was haunted by negativity and
    wickedness,
And when we failed and people died, their meanings to us
    did not make sense.

Most of us were shown how to fight, lie and steal,
That we didn't even hesitate to think twice when it was time
    to kill.

Our minds were so corrupted that now we're proud of the life
    that we represent;
But our ignorance is so great that when consequences come
    to life we just cannot comprehend.

We run around stealing and killing in our already poor
    communities,
That when we get put in jail for our stupidity, we blame the
    authorities.

But when the questions come and they wonder why we act
this way,
Our lack of knowledge and intelligence catches up to us and
we have nothing in return to say.

Some of us make excuses and find ways to explain why we
live the way we do,
But nobody would ever tell you what's real or what's really
true.

The sad thing about this is that this cycle keeps going on
without any intention of coming to a conclusion.
And the longer it goes, the more young lives we end up
losing.

I, myself, am part of this cycle and I'm still in this life that
has given me the most crucial ride,
But now finding a purpose to life because of where I come
from, there's nowhere I can find some pride!

Escape

Ramón Escobar
Inside Out Writers

Sometimes life gets a little too rough,
Sometimes we feel as if we've had enough.

Sometimes we get overcrowded by situations too hard to
    understand,
So we let them dictate our paths 'cause their meanings we
    cannot comprehend.

Sometimes we're overshadowed by our hates and fears,
So we pray to God for guidance with seldom tears.

Sometimes we speak anger with harsh words we mean not to
    say,
Sometimes we get mad 'cause things don't go our way.

Sometimes we let our emotions get in the way of our destiny,
Because we're blinded by fantasy, and too scared of reality.

Sometimes we lock ourselves in our own little jail,
We take away our minds' freedom and put it in a prison cell.

Sometimes we just get tired of our own corruption,
Which leads us to our own self-destruction.

Sometimes we wish our problems, worries and cares would
    just disappear,
Along with our pain, sorrows and worst all, fears.

So we try to find a passageway out of this mess,
But in reality it is from ourselves from whom we are running
away.

Sometimes we wonder what we're searching from, our fate,
But the only answer is that we're looking for an ESCAPE!

Hopeless

Ramón Escobar
Inside Out Writers

My ignorant ways of life are something I will never forget,
Living with a guilty conscience and now suffering with pain
    is all I ever set.

Just now sitting here and thinking of everything I've done,
Makes me feel disgusted of what I thought of as fun.

What else am I to do now that I am a habilitated person?
If my past is building my future and my life seems to worsen?

Now it's just me and four walls that my kind have forced the
    world to build,
To make me realize and experience my own simple guilt.

I tried to lay back and accept that this is where I belong,
But my heart couldn't agree and rots dead with my wrongs.

My emotions tried fighting out of the cage I once made,
The cage I once built by the game I now play.

I looked all around and saw no one could help me,
Which makes me feel lonely and inside really empty.

I tried keeping my head up so that I won't be too weak,
But I can't understand what I'm trying to seek.

I focused on the right to find a better solution,
But now I've tried that and the reaction was a negative con-
    clusion.

I tried to do the opposite of what I once used to be,
But from this angle it looks like I'll never be free.

There's no way for me to keep moving on,
Because I'm still in this place in which they say I belong.

I've tried every way and everything that I could,
But my only way out is to go the way I promised I never
    once again would.

I'm getting real lost and on my own is how I now feel,
Weaker and weaker wishing my destruction wasn't real.

Now I've reached my lowest point and with the sick I have
    ended,
Realizing that my only chance, I've already spent it.

I'm not sure how I've concluded with such evil state of mind,
But I do know that my innocence, my peace and emotions
    have all been left behind.

I can't find a reason to change my mentality, to keep moving
    on,
And my patience and hopes seem to now be all gone.

As my life seems to hit rock bottom and I feel like I am near
    my death,
I look back at my life and realize that sadly I feel as if I have
    nothing left.

So now I say good-bye to the ones that I love,
And hopefully there's no hard feelings once we meet up
    above!

Somebody, Please!

Ramón Escobar
Inside Out Writers

Somebody, please hear me,
Take a minute to see.

Somebody, please look at my misery,
Understand my crying agony.

Somebody, please take a minute,
Don't look out, but in it.

Somebody, please let me explain,
And let me pour out my pain.

Somebody, please don't judge,
Or hold a devilish grudge.

Somebody, please hear my story,
Of shame with no glory.

Somebody, please look at my cry,
But please don't ask why.

Somebody, please give me strength,
To give my undeserving life length.

Somebody, please forgive the sins,
The ones deep within.

Somebody, please don't hate this one,
This one of death with no shining sun.

Somebody, please . . .
Somebody, please . . .

The Future

Ramón Escobar
Inside Out Writers

Will my life ever have a future? I ask this to myself over and
over;
Because these cell bricks make me feel like I'm going nowhere.

My mind, at times, runs to my future and tries to dictate
what's ahead;
But doesn't come back with a positive answer because of this
life that I led.

My regrets and sorrows are begging to please be forgiven;
For the wrong actions and negativity I once chose to live in.

But that decision was made way before I discovered myself;
And before I didn't have any feeling or even cared about my
living wealth.

Now that I've come to my senses it's so hard for me to understand my mistakes;
And to accept that there's ways to change my life's fate.

I'm only seventeen and wonder if I will make it to twenty-
four,
But by the way I visualize my life at the moment I just don't
know.

Inside I would love and work for so much more than what I
have now;
But that reality is almost slim and unknown if it will be
bound.

Words of a Soldier

Ramón Escobar
Inside Out Writers

So here I go, coming clean, confessing all of my sins,
And most of the bad things
That have been tormenting my life's dreams.

My life has not been so good,
Living nothing but the 'hood,
With a corrupted mentality like if I have should.

Not caring, where to live or die,
And in my mind all I thought was a ride
With the support of my Mexican pride.

But Damn! Here I am once again,
Looking for my so-called friends
That I thought would ride with me to the end.

Shit! I guess I was wrong,
Being ignorant for listening to that song,
That I interpreted as if this is where I belong.

Look at me, I'm sinking,
Not knowing what I'm thinking,
And wishing that my actions were as smart as I am speaking.

And now, I feel I have nothing left but this cell,
A body that has been through hell,
And a mind, heart and spirit that will prevail!

Freedom Is a Battlefield

Cruz J. Ramírez (Juan Cañizales)
Homies Unidos

Freedom is a battlefield
A constant struggle
between two opposing forces.
Soldiers on both sides courageous,
believers, willful, loyal to their side.
The remnants of old scars
gash the fields past,
deep trenches on the soil
where the soldiers take refuge
from their enemies,
one of their own.
But beyond the smoke of battle
beyond their sight
is room for movement,
room to advance.
Whoever decides to move,
to overcome fear and
meet face to face
with those opposing,
will realize our true fate.
Meeting eye to eye, mind to mind.

The Night

Cruz J. Ramírez (Juan Cañizales)
Homies Unidos

The night is full of screams
From ear to ear
Forehead
To the back of my head
The high pitches
Of my mother's expectations
The low pitches
Of my father's disappointments
The playful laughs
Of my sisters that I ignore
Seeking a resolution
My own voice whispers
Underneath it all

Seeking approval
My voice begins to fade
A dim light
Consumed by my thoughts
Thoughts of others.

Giants

Cruz J. Ramírez (Juan Cañizales)
Homies Unidos

Among Giants
I am among giants
Their feet rooted
To the same ground
I walk on
Their bodies absorbing
The same air

Let me reach
Your height
Let me see
Your view
Beyond the giants
Towering over me
Let me be
Your equal

Who Could Have Known

Cruz J. Ramírez (Juan Cañizales)

Homies Unidos

Hold your head up high
You'll make it through
Try to focus on the sky
Watch the stars explode
As you keep hold
Steady now

This is the moment of truth
No help is on the way
Bruised and fatigue
Tortured and healed
Your wounds
May never seal

The gaping whole
In the middle of your chest
Will consume you
Leaving you empty
And wanting more
For your soul

The pain is too familiar
Keep pushing it away
This is something
That wishes to stay
Underneath your skin
Burning, eating
Your foundation

No one knows what
Could have taken my motivation
But here I am
Motionless, petrified
Who could of known
I could lose my motivation?

Thoughtful

Anthony Querubín

CURYJ

San Francisco Jail #5 at San Bruno, CA

It was a hot summer night
just rockin' an' rollin' in my 745LI
Enjoying the freedoms of the U.S.A.
Feeling like a king,
a lion,
determined to shine
Shine like a diamond, but
stay solid as a rock,
Thinking before I sell my soul
for that green, I will lose
everything.

Reflection

Jorge Mestayer

CURYJ

San Francisco Jail #5 at San Bruno, CA

The rainy weather comes
crashing down
on the hillside that is my life

The brown puddles
that form are sweat and tears
that fall
from my skin

Like the taste
of a bitter pear
I wake
up at noon
on a work day
and find it comical

Brown Dreams

Juan Guardado
CURYJ

I guess I got those not-so-brown, brown dreams
The ones that stuck to me like the those thorny things I
    picked up on
my shoelaces and pant legs when we played in the overgrown
    weeds
I'm having trouble trying to see
If these dreams are really mine
Searching between half-cast memories and inner longing
    that divides me
These dreams where I play my biggest enemy and am only
    held back by my
own fear of accomplishment
In these brown dreams I'm scared
like a child left to fend for himself in a crowd of unfamiliar
    faces like I'm not supposed to be here

Like a child I grab my arms and wrap them around my knees
I hold tight feeling the warm breath bounce off of my passed-
    down
denim and slowly peek through the cracks in my fingers.
I see the faces of grown men postured and perceiving
And the inquisitive eyes of women and children questioning
    my presence as if to ask are you one of us? but they all
    belong
Synchronized like the rhythmic background music.
Their souls pulse to rhythm foreign and strong

Their pride permeating like the scent of the food that creeps
    through the hallways

But crouched in my fearful stance I get the feeling like I'm
    not welcome
But I've got nowhere else to go

You see, my brown dreams are different from others.
They're not painted on barrio walls or captured in symbolic
    phases
cascaded over conga drums
They are not idolatrized in movies where played-out actors
    play out roles of played-out images of homeboys
They are not graced by the presence of romantic poems and
    heartfelt corridos that rise from the depths of one's stom-
    ach and belt out the feelings trapped inside

My brown dreams are silenced.
muted by a tongue unable to pronounce the words
commanded by the ears that can barely understand
and moved by the body that knows it should do what it's told
    if it can only figure out what that is.

You see my brown dreams can become nightmares if dreamt
    on the wrong night.
how can you be brown when there is so much white fading
    your color?
I've come to the painful realization that it's an
exclusive club on both sides and I haven't been invited to
    either
It takes a lot of white to fade brown down to a tan

But even a drop of brown can be noticed on an all-white
    canvas
One look in the other direction and I'm quickly assured that
    I'm on the right side of the tracks

'Cause my dreams are brown for a reason . . . and ever since I
   could remember it's been that way.

Even though I never could repeat what he was saying
I took the stage every time Richie came on
And as I trot across my father's couch singing "para bailar la
   bamba" . . .
With my brown belly sticking over my elastic mc hammer
   pants
They used to belong to my big brother and will soon belong
   to my younger brother 'cause that's the way we did shit

And I would bang the car dashboard just like my father as he
   sang salsa tunes out the window of his multicolored Ford
   Escort with a brown paper bag he picked up from the corner store stashed behind the driver's seat.

And from the day I was born he was called Papi to Paps to
   Papa . . .
and I had more tías than I'd ever had aunts or uncles
and I might not be able to talk about it but I could damn
   sure say my vowels with an accent.

A.E.I.O.U.

and my forests were always jungles and my lakes were always
   oceans and
my mountains were volcanoes.

And the city to me
was la mission and la parque dolores before the hipsters and
   gay people.

My brown dreams always had the right backdrop
I just felt like I wasn't the right actor

But the more I dreamt them the more I could to see
that peering through those lightly tinted brown fingers was a
    boy
trapped in his own nightmare
Afraid that I wasn't brown enough I never went outside and
    got a tan.

Sometimes we just need a little light to bring the brown out
So those thorny things still stick to my pants as I race across
    the
overgrown weeds, and those songs still play from the second
    story
windows as I walk through my neighborhood

That's where I know why all the homeboys say
it's all about getting down with the getdown.

New Dreams, Visions and Horizons

Johnny Howe
Santa Cruz Barrios Unidos Prison Project

I can remember back when I was a young boy
I wasn't interested in sports, games or the latest toy.
I remember thinking about joining a gang and selling drugs
It seemed like all I ever really wanted was to be a thug.
I was willing to do whatever I could just to fit in.
Even if that meant killing someone and going to the pen
Looking back I never realized how low was my self-esteem
And how I would try to hide it by acting mean.
At the age of 17 I remember walking into court.
I looked around and had absolutely no support.
I had always believed that the homies would always be there
Now that I have just got sentenced to life I couldn't find one
    anywhere.

So now on my way to prison I go
With my old distorted beliefs and still willing to go with the
    flow.
I'm still doing the same things I was doing on the streets
20 years later, involved in gangs, doing drugs and feeling the
    heat.
I know I need to change my beliefs if I want to get out.
At 40 years old, I'm finally learning what life is really about.
It's not about being selfish, hurting others or throwing away
    your life.
It's about being of service, starting a family and having a wife.
It's about walking on the beach, enjoying life and having fun.
I now know it's not about trying to impress others or carrying
    a gun.
As I lay back and allow myself to dream in this empty cell

The one thing I know for sure is I no longer want to die in
this hell.
Now I dream about helping others who have the problems I
had
Showing them that their dreams and visions don't have to be
sad.
Explaining to others that the choices they make can be their
own.
That they don't have to come to prison and make it their
permanent home.
I now understand that change starts in the mind
I look back and realize that I was so blind.
I hold onto my new dream of finally being free
Even though I haven't taken one step out of this penitentiary.
My new vision is of being at the beach lying in the sun
It's no longer about why I got an extra five years for possession
of a gun.
As I watch the horizon through these prison bars,
I remind myself to never stop reaching for the stars.

Anger, Confusion, Loneliness, Fear

Scott Dean Russo
Santa Cruz Barrios Unidos
Santa Cruz Juvenile Hall

Angry at myself, the police, my probation officer
Confused about my life and who I have become
What I stand for, what I believe in
Lonely, alone, by myself in here
New faces, I miss my family
Fear of doing a lot of time
Fear of looking weak
Fear of fear
I can't blame anyone for making me feel these feelings
No one put a gun in my hand
Or a knife and told me to fight
No one forced me to use drugs or break the law
Who am I?
What do I stand for?
Where are my friends now?
Where are my homies now?
What is real?
What is real is that we don't have to feel this way
We don't have to be a slave to drugs, gangs and the system
We can have a real meaning for life!

Wishing I Was Free

JB

Santa Cruz Barrios Unidos
Santa Cruz Juvenile Hall

I'm gonna keep it real
And tell you what I feel
Tired of these cold bricks and steel.
They try to offer me a deal
But they are crazy to me
It means no appeal!
Wishing I could fly away
Day after day
Wishing I was free
Enjoying the sunshine
With my friends and family

¿Hasta Cuándo?

Javier "Xavier" Haro
Santa Cruz Barrios Unidos
Soledad Prison

Young homie
For many years now
A senseless war has been raging on
Behind prison walls
And throughout Aztlán.
A war between our barrios
And known brothers
A war between numbers
And gang colors . . .
. . . Raza killing raza!!
¡Hasta cuándo?

And after all these years
And after all the tears
What have we achieved so far?
How much blood has been spilled?
How many dreams have been killed?
How many coffins have been filled?
And after all that's been said
And after all that's been done.
The violence rages on and on.
How many more mothers must cry?
How many more years must go by?
Before we realize it's self-genocide
Are we so blind that we can't see?
Open your eyes before it's too late
The Divide and Conquer Tactic is Still in Effect!

Young homie,
The time we lay down our weapons of hate
And learn to live with peace and respect,
It's time we end the violence
For the good of mankind!
It's time we unveiled
For the good of Aztlán!
It's time we moved forward
To reclaim our title
"The people of the sun."

United we stand, divided we fall!!!

Blind Warrior

Javier "Xavier" Haro
Santa Cruz Barrios Unidos
Soledad Prison

Blind Warriors, wandering the streets of night
They don't know how the war began
Or when it's ever going to end
They just go around instead, tripping on each other
Brother against brother, waging war
For all the world to see

Blind Warriors, living in a dark world
Playing shoot 'em up bang bang
On the edge of life and death
Motivated by false pride and revenge
They sacrifice honor for shame
Putting in work for the game
All in the name of the street gang

Blind Warriors on the battlefield of life
Led by deception they take up arms
Marching down the path of destruction
Raza unity is left behind, distrust is relied upon
Reason is abandoned to a warped state of mind
Nothing makes sense to them anymore

Not even the calling of conch, flutes, rattles or drum
These have guided the Mexicayotl through their battles

Blind Warriors fighting without a cause
Drawing weapons out to strike each other down
One by one they fall at the hands of their own kind
One by one they fall, inside coffins or a prison cell
Nothing became of the war games
Nothing will remain of their nicknames
Just another rest in peace on a wall or grave stone
Just another teardrop that will fall.

Enemy

Geraldo "Monkey" Martínez
Santa Cruz Barrios Unidos

Within confinement it all began . . . combated explosions-
furious roar!
Swinging-moving-ducking as if there's a strive to survive.
True battle had begun!
Sweat-anxiety-energized power as I confront my enemy.
Eye-to-eye . . . I see the strain in his gaze. Peering deep with
a power
That can't be seen. I'm locking in a struggle in life, spirit and
dreams!
Who will survive . . . who will give in . . . I've seen the
bleeding
Caused by him, the pain he created. True pain he's given.
True stress
He has lived, shed in rage and inner pain held in. Impulsive
Unmanaged reaction to the unseen. I'm in a hand-to-hand
rumble with
No end! Getting hit! . . . Feeling the hurt he's inflicted . . .
His fear has
Made him strong! With burst of adrenaline knocking me
down. My
Mind at a daze . . . tears cascade . . .
When did this accrue?
The day I truly saw myself in a mirror. Not just as a reflec-
tion, but as
The enemy. Not just as a reflection, but as the enemy
within . . .
Who has a horrific turmoil

Was where my mind-heart emotions-spirit were
Twisting like a hurricane.
But . . . once I had control,
I see no enemy no more
I see calmness in his smile.
A sincere hug to say be happy you're alive
Share by how you strive to live. 'Cause what you give is your
    total
Reflection, outer and in . . . now my enemy has become my
    best friend.
Staying balance-walking in the awareness of my humanity
    . . . with
What I've learned I've found
The sincerity of my smile.

Superhero: Past-Present-Future

Geraldo "Monkey" Martínez
Santa Cruz Barrios Unidos

I have found out, I have super powers . . . Just like the char-
    acters in
Comic books and movies.
It was strange because "They've" always been there. All I had to
Do was realize . . . to pick it up and place it on.
Yes . . . my abilities! That make me unique . . . really . . .
    makes us all
Unique.
Oh . . . you don't know? You also have the qualities of
    becoming
A superhero!
My abilities come from a cape that sways and floats with the
Wind while I move forward
I've attached my powers . . . ready to fly . . .
Can you see me . . . not that I wanted to be noticed or want
    you to
Look. But if my heart were sincere my deeds would go to
    your eyes.
So . . . now I smile.
Knowing that to a bad mood I am like Kryptonite.
So much power-strength-knowledge my cape carries.
Keeping me humble understanding with pride!
The good kind . . .
That's how I know I'm a superhero.
My cape is the past that powers my strength
Bringing me an understanding-knowledge-wisdom as I like
    in the present has made me prepared for almost every-
    thing.
So, now you and I know: superheroes last as long as we need
    them.

Apágalo
Freddie Gutiérrez
CURYJ

Turn off the noise
hear us, ancestor

we remember you—remember when I first wrote
        first wrote you back into existence
because with pen, flame plume in hand
we conjure that consciousness that burns
beneath our faces
      the pilot of being
      manifesting fire essence

we conjure what burns
a fire in the chest
the burning of accordion fold books
folding inheritance of the old-old pen dance
in trance we write
mystified by hand motions
penning the pressures of gravity
as we gravitate towards the margins
expanding literal
pushed syntax—pushing the limits of diction
recalling mindsets and lifeviews
before the men with helmets
crowned our domes

remember?

I remember when I wrote myself home
sick with the eager epidemic
        for the right to return
to highlight in sunshine
the journey towards purpose
with our homelands in our hearts

we beat our chest before we speak
it's loud and clear
        we step in front of our former selves
as former slaves away from our cells

Thunder Cats

Freddie Gutiérrez
CURYJ

Cats with the thunder in their voice box
a rumble in the throat
beast mode forward
for the word
a quick strike of the pen
beckoning the voice of the barrio
call of the hood

cats with the thunder in their voice box
call it cornerstone folklore
scribes of the concrete petroglyphs
American artists who rock well
with sunshine cool in their back pockets

cats with the thunder in their voice box
Sharpie garras leaving their mark on the cement thickets
real grillo poetas
artistas of el mero-mero Alurista
sun risa raza roja

63 Impala

Freddie Ramírez
CURYJ

The stuff   (ether strut)
young homeboys' dreams are made of
fantasized rides
            tumbao
                    low
                            low
                                    low
Polished chrome
scraping asphalt
those days it's no faults
    all day play

Creased
from white tee shoulders
down
to khaki cuffs

49 Fleetline

Freddie Ramírez
CURYJ

The Blue Bomb
fattest white walls
skirts
Cherry Bomb Glass Pack exhaust

Sundays only
everyone's dolled up
Papi wears Ray Bans
Mami's got on carmine lipstick
I'm wearing suspenders
Sister Girl with a ruffled dress and Little Bo Peep hat

Sundays only
no one ever talks in this car
feels like we're all pretending something

Like Wind in Our Veins

Freddie Gutiérrez
CURYJ

Writing is the way
we communicate
      our needs
      our fears
      our hearts
bleed ink
drop words like blows
like wind in our veins

yeah it hurts
esta responsabilidad duele
pero arrancamos
el camino de los poetas
dragging the past into us, as we stand eternal at the cusp of
    the future,
in thrust in the midst of the present

lashing pen strokes on maguey
splashing backstrokes to the way
       etching writing

como trancazos sobre la espalda vieja
de nuestro ancestro: el Indio,
arms spread to gather the tools of inscription
juntando la memoria comunal del tlacuilo
el que escribe, escarba y carga la palabra

pariéndonos la madre tierra
tierra bajo nuestras uñas

de uña y carne oramos
himnos dignos
          Xikiyehua in xochitl
Xikiyehua in xochitl
Xikiyehua in moyojlo
pampa nimitstlasotla
pampa nimitstlasotla
ika nochi noyojlo

que duelen
dentro del proceso
del recordar
de la memoria celular

My Name Is Justice

Frank de Jesús Acosta

My name is justice,
   I am everyone's child
I am yours to nurture, protect
   & bring to a higher being
Love is my mother,
   the womb of my birth & lifeblood
Faith is my father,
   fire spirit of creation that we all share
Tribe is my family, community
   the confluence of relations across humanity
The earth is our home,
   a gift from Creator to share not possess
The tree of life roots us in virtue,
   respect, dignity, compassion & magnanimity
The branches are equity,
   compassion, forgiveness, reckoning, reconciliation
Our being is inter-connected:
   in-jury, in-conflict, in-justice, in-love, in-harmony
Walk in a sacred manner,
   our beginning & our eternity is in the heart of God

Healing Prayer at the Tree of Life

Frank de Jesús Acosta

I prayed before the tree of life
Breathing heart to heart
These humble tears of gratitude
A circle of souls bound by love
Welcomes, farewells, heartache, joy
Blessings have benevolent demands

I prayed before the living tree
The presence of mothers and sisters
Fathers lost and parents gained
Anguish of losing those we love
Discovery and union of kindred souls
Children unborn, conceived, espoused

Wars waged in greed, moot divisions of creed
Prisons of hate, blood, flesh, iron and stone
Injured roots, ailing tree, a wounded human family
Truth, forgiveness, justice, healing inter-connectedness
Family, friends, strangers, enemies transformed
Tribal relations restores, the gathering of nations

Remember Me Now

Frank de Jesús Acosta

My dreams take me to the edge of love
Only the penumbra of beauty finds my vision
So I dance in the sunlight as best I can
I am the thirsty, hungry and destitute child
The neglected on the forsaken places of earth
My curse is to be born unworthy; beyond dignity
Where pale bestows hegemony, birthright, privilege
Where a cup of milk and few grains of rice
Are as scarce as a touch of compassion, grace
Corporate science has shrunk the world a Twitter
Rendering me invisible in the eyes of profit
Expendable in a world of waste, gluttony, self-gratification
Neighbors in a world of want, famine and deprivation
Race renders me pariah; aborting me to poverty
Demonized; reared at the breast of desperation; self-loathing
I become a beast to be caged, forgotten: death by nihilism
When the healing touch of love and cultura could save me
Pigment condemns me unworthy of truth, accountability,
    redemption
Born beyond the touch of forgiveness, redemption, human
    kindness
I pray in passing to spirit, to return as waters of benevolence
That my bones become fodder on sovereign fertile soils
So my enduring love may nourish the neglected of earth
May my muted song today unheard by so many
Flourish as a symphony of kinship shared among nations
I am the sod, seed and fruit of the tree of humanity
I am God's child forgotten . . . Remember me now . . .

On Blue Days (Love Reconciles)

Frank de Jesús Acosta

On blue days like these
I see beyond the stars
Where all children grow old
Never knowing violence, wars
On blue days like these
I see endless grain fields
Sovereign groves laden with fruit
Common feasts with no one left out
Blue days like these
Attest harmony as our truest being
A bond, rhythm and accord
Heartbeat of all living things
Blue days give us wings
Ascendance to dance with the spirits
We are reborn in flight to drumbeats
Culture songs, poems and prayers
Dancing together as one sacred circle
Blue days are not without pain
Intimate knowledge of suffering
Scars bear witness to shared wounds
Those we've caused, those suffered
Amid prevalence of cruelty and egoism
Eyes of the poor weeping crimson
Yet all that ails must succumb
Curative powers of faith and compassion
On blue days like these
Blood, water, fire, spirit, wind, breath
Heaven and earth become one with the Creator
A reflection of all that we can become
In kinship, humanity, love fulfilled

Nine Skins of a Cat: Barrio Reflections

Frank de Jesús Acosta

I look to the past through the eyes of incredulity
Cloaked in the armor of intrepid youth
I lived as the cat in its first six skins
Preservation instincts; I prowled my concrete jungle
By the power of maternal prayer, I survive
Every mêlée, blade and bullet, near mortal wound
Each willful wrong imparted or exacted; reckoning waits
A cage concrete, steal, shackles, silent tears
Wading in toxic waters amid flowerless thorns
Leaving an indelible mark; demanding their toll
A cat in its 7th skin, face to face with my own duplicity
Lessons of injustice and restorative grace, a dichotomy
Looking at the present thru the greying eyes of adulthood
I am the cat in his 8th skin, learning to walk more humbly
Skins shed in epochs; fault, remorse, reconciliation & gratitude
I see the wrinkled praying hands of my sacred mother
Cleansed in the fire of revelation & tears of healing absolution
Healed in a circle of human kindness & love unconditional
I offer a contrite and resurrect heart to an ailing world
My 9th skin will be that of love inspired wisdom & service
My eyes a window to a seven-generation journey
Seeking to honor our living circle & the seven generations
   to follow

If I Could Go Home . . .

Adrián

Middle school student at Met West School Refugee
and Migrants Summer Program
CURYJ

If I could go back home
I wouldn't go alone,
I would go as I came
with the same bones.

Poema de la amistad

Jesús
Middle school student at Met West School Refugee
and Migrants Summer Program
CURYJ

Si la amistad fuera una guerra
yo y todos mis amigos
¡acabaríamos con el mundo!

Poem of Friendship

If friendship was a war
me and all of my friends
would end the world!

La rosita

Jorge
Middle school student at Met West School Refugee
and Migrants Summer Program
CURYJ

"¡Hey, locos, párenle!"

vi unos batos tratando de destruir una rosa
les dije que le pararan
que dejaran la rosita en paz
porque esa rosa podía crecer fuerte
linda y hermosa.

The Little Rose

Hey, homies, stop!

I saw some homeboys trying to destroy a rose
I told them to stop it,
to leave the little rose in peace
for that rose can grow up strong
lovely and beautiful.

Mis amigos

Hugo
Middle school student at Met West School Refugee
and Migrants Summer Program
CURYJ

mis amigos y yo
no queremos ir a la guerra
porque preferimos jugar
pero mis amigos y yo
no nos vamos a dejar agarrar.

My Friends

My friends and I
we don't want to go to war
We prefer to play
so my friends and I
will not let ourselves be caught.

Suit of Manhood

Freddy Gutiérrez
CURYJ

I inherited the workingman's boot step from the treaded earth hillsides of Yahualica, Jalisco. It was there my grandfather Manuel swung machetes to cut open maguey and gather honey water to make pulque in orange clay pots picked up by my grandfather Alfredo when they left their motherland to chase the American Dream in the City of Angels. That is where my pops wore wool Pendleton's striped with machismo bad habits in his heart side pocket.

The first and only time my father took me shopping to the mall we saw this red block, grey-lined and cream-tinged Pendleton in Gottschalks.

He said, "This is the real deal, homey."

He bought the shirt and a pair of khaki Dickies for me. He taught me how to crease them up, razor-blade straight, slicing the breeze with each regal step, like a beautiful jaguar.

I wore white tee, Hanes—the 3-packs, affordable, always tucked in, pants never lower than the waist line, leaning back with a serpentine spine sitting nice in the pocket of our waists.

My pops still wears his Dickies, especially when he goes out. I still wear mine, especially when I go outside to do work. I don't trip about creasing them up anymore, and I don't really try to walk like my father does, but I try to work as hard as he and the men in our family that came before me have.

I've not bought a Pendleton since that one that my pops gave me. But almost every time that I look into my closet, I swear I see it hanging on the pole in the corner of my eye, just like every time I wear my Dickies I swear I walk spring-step-switch-blade-gangsta-lean, regal, like a beautiful jaguar treading the concrete—regal, like my pops.

Untitled

Ramón Escobar, Jr.
Inside/Out Writers

South Central, Los Angeles is the community that I called home growing up. Born into a dysfunctional family, I quickly began following my family traditions, becoming a product of my environment at a very young age. The childhood memories that I now have all involve the presence of violence, drugs and illegal activity that seemed to be normal in my neighborhood as well as home. I grew up believing that the things I was seeing and experiencing were the norm or the only things life had to offer. My decisions and aspirations in life were largely influenced by this perspective and quickly landed me in front of a judge by the age of ten, when I was placed into a special anti-gang program and given probation.

At twelve years old, I had become a full active gang member and an asset to the "family business." It did not take long for me to violate probation, committing a crime that resulted in sentencing to juvenile hall detention and placement at Juvenile Probation Camp Challenger, a dreadful place where the word "rehabilitation" did not exist. Serving my time in this institution can be likened to attending a criminal finishing school. I learned the negative anti-social behaviors it takes to survive while "graduating with honors" among my peers and family. After serving my sentence, I was released and within hours of walking out of the courtroom, I found myself

93

back in my old neighborhood, back in my old home and behind the trigger of a gun. Once again, the same day I was released, I violated my probation for another crime.

The Juvenile Court stripped me of my rights as a minor and immediately remanded me to adult court to face a life sentence. I was on the fast track, only fourteen years old and facing a fifty years to life term of incarceration. Reality set in as all I could think of was the prospect of going to adult prison to join the relatives and friends I knew awaited me. One night, while being detained in a transitional detention compound (Barry J. Nidorf Juvenile Hall in Sylmar, CA), awaiting one of my many court dates, a probation officer announced that there would be a voluntary writers' class in ten minutes and to be ready to step out when called if we wanted to attend.

I had never thought about writing but I wanted to get out of my cell, as being in constant lockdown was getting old quick. I walked into class and immediately started goofing around with some peers until this white guy teaching by the name of Scott Budnick started to quiet us down to begin his lesson. All of my peers started to write, and I just sat there, staring at the blank page, not feeling a thing nor caring about this white guy wasting his time with us. Scott came up to me and started to ask why I didn't give it a try. My reply was, "I don't care about your class, don't care about writing, and I'm about to get life in prison, so what's the point?" Scott continued to try and encourage my ignorant young mind to take a chance, but I just ignored him and didn't write at all.

That night, it was really hard for me to sleep and my mind was racing a million miles an hour. I thought about the white guy from earlier that day. I felt I had disrespected him and the class, so I got off my bed, reached for a pencil and paper and started flooding the lines. Ten pages later, I was out of paper and at 2 am I interrupted the probation staff's nap for some more sheets. A couple of days later when the class was held, I walked up to the teacher and apologized for my rudeness and handed him some twenty pages telling the story of my four-teen-year trek to incarceration. From that moment on, not only did Scott Budnick become my teacher, but also a mentor, role model and that big brother everyone wishes they had as a kid. Scott continued to teach the Inside/Out Writers class and was determined to expand my mind from the mental barriers and life defeating values that had been instilled in me since I was a born. It took more than a few years for the seeds that he was planting in me to start finally blossoming. I was sen-tenced, sent out to serve some time in California Youth Authority (C.Y.A.), now known as the Division of Juvenile Justice (D.J.J.). Upon turning eighteen, I was sent to Chino, a California State Adult Prison. It took a couple of more felonies for me to finally realize that the dead-end life that I was so consumed by, and the loyalty I had towards its false beliefs and value system, were all a lie.

Through the years and stints in multiple facilities dating back to childhood, I was literally being raised in the criminal justice system. Scott became a constant positive presence. He would pop up out of the blue in front of my cell at times when I needed him most; send the most random letters filled with words of wisdom and hope in dark times; and was always that someone outside my cell who believed in me even when I didn't believe in myself. On my last term of detention, I served my time in the Los Angeles County Jail under a bill called AB109. While in this facility, I was lucky to be placed in a school dorm, where I chose to become a positive influence over my peers and really transform my way of living. I initiat-ed and facilitated developmental classes, advocated for more educational resources and soon was collaborating with other inmates to teach one another. In fact, we started the first

Inside/Out Writers class offered in an adult detention facility. During this period, I continued to work in preparation towards my release and re-entry into family, community and society.

Today, I am a father of two beautiful girls and have transformed in ways that were once unimaginable to me. I have continued to play a huge role in the Inside/Out Writers program as well as the Anti-Recidivism Coalition. In many ways, writing saved me, opening my heart to healing culture, finding a new truth and values to guide my life, giving me a purpose of believing in people that are currently in the same situation and state of mind I once occupied. I now truly value the opportunities after so much negativity that played out in my young life. Currently, I'm a full time student seeking to gain my business degree, continuing to mentor people who are currently incarcerated or recently released to help them re-enter society, and advocating for restorative centered juvenile justice. I was also given an opportunity by another great friend, teacher and mentor, Todd Rubenstein, and have been employed at an Entertainment Law Firm in Century City, California, where I have been embraced, constantly learning new things and continuing to freely expand my mind as far as it can go.

To My Brothers in Confinement

Javier "Xavier" Haro
Santa Cruz Barrios Unidos
Soledad Prison

Greetings! My name is Xavier and I am writing you from the place of solitude (a.k.a. Soledad Prison). If you're a gangster following in my footsteps or an individual living a similarly destructive lifestyle, then you are going to trip out on this. What I have to share is something that would have changed the course of my life. More importantly, it would have saved a person's life. It was a moment in time that would have prevented a lot of tears, suffering and pain.

Three days before my life went down this hellhole, I was going to make a life-changing decision—a decision I had come to right after the birth of my son about six months back. To avoid all that mushy stuff, let's just say his birth was an awesome experience and witnessing his first breath of life was the happiest moment of my life. It didn't take long to realize what I had to do: let my homies know I was retiring from the gang life so I could focus on being a dad. I thought it would be easy, but for some reason it was hard to tell people I grew up with that I was calling it quits, that I was moving on with my life. So as the days, weeks and months went by, I just kept putting it off.

It wasn't until after Christmas that I decided to finally break the news. The homies in my clique were looking to do something for New Year's Day, so I proposed a barbeque at the park. For them, it was just another get together to celebrate the New Year. For me, it was going to be the end of a lifestyle and the beginning of a new way of life. Even though I was still young (I had just turned nineteen), I felt like they would understand my decision and respect me for it. But when the moment came to make my announcement, I could not find the words to say what I needed to say. The courage I had when I faced my so-called enemies failed me in front of my childhood friends. Three days later I was involved in a gang-related shooting that ended a young man's life and left another two injured. As a result of my terrible actions, the judge served me real good with multiple life sentences. Twenty-one years later I'm still in the pen, not knowing when or if I'll ever get out again.

It's been a long and difficult journey since then. A journey filled with misery and pain, stress, frustration and regrets, and above all fear—fear of the unknown, fear that surrounds us and resides inside us all.

Since my incarceration, I have sat in a cell questioning my life and thinking how different it would be today if I had left that lifestyle behind. Why did I chicken out that night in the park? What was I afraid of? Why did I choose to continue on a destructive path instead of a productive one? Those are just some of the questions that have haunted my mind day and night. I used to think it was because my homeboys still needed me, that I couldn't leave them hanging at a time when the fighting was increasing. But that's all bull! They were just excuses I made up to justify my actions, to hide the root cause of my failure or inability to change. As much as I hate to admit this, fear played a bigger role. My hood and my homeboys were my comfort zone. So in reality, I was scared of letting go, of going outside that comfort zone and facing the world on my own.

Looking back, I regret a lot of things I did or didn't do, like putting off my decision to move on with my life, not being there for my son. I regret my actions that killed another human being. Putting my family through all this bull crap, dropping out of high school, giving up my dreams and goals . . . If I could turn back time to undo all the pain and suffering I caused, I would do it in an instant, but nothing can change the past. All I can do is change myself: my negative lifestyle, my attitude, outlook on life and the path that led me here. And all I have left besides the days ahead of me (which by the way are not guaranteed) is some hope, my family's love and support, the will to keep on living, a desire to better myself, help others and, if possible, make it home someday.

I hope my experience gives you something to think about, and if there is a lesson here, then may you figure it out before you end up like me, or worse, before it's too late. Stay strong and keep your spirits up.

With respect, Xavier

I Was Asked . . .

Geraldo "Monkey" Martínez
Santa Cruz Barrios Unidos Prison Project

I was asked, "If you had the opportunity to go back in time and could tell your seventeen-year-old self anything, what would you tell him/her?"

"If, before I started to fall deeper from my future in my partially made hole, I was able to receive a message from my future, it would have been, "Listen to your heart, caring is who you really are even though you're seventeen and life has been hard. Don't let your eyes deceive you. That gut feeling is telling you what you're up to, or there is trouble ahead. Keep that desire to learn, to be happy. Don't try to mirror someone who doesn't even care for himself, much less care about you. You know who you are, be proud in a good way of your DNA, down the line from mom and dad. Listen but also hear and feed all words, good or bad. One can learn from everything—just don't get caught up in the sensationalizing of what others do, say or have. You are persistent and that will help you in achieving your goals. That smile, people appreciate it, because it is felt with a sincere openness. Don't let anyone deter you from your true passion. There is much to see and learn; choose wisely for short-term or long-term goals. Life is what we make of it and whom we share it with. Be patient, especially with relationships, where emotions can be sometimes overwhelming. Let your mind, heart and spirit strengthen your journey and become a real man, not by word, but by character and action of how you walk in life. Be humane."

If I received a message from myself at seventeen, after the arrest, it would have been:

"You are seventeen. Your journey will be filled with rough times—emotional, physical and spiritual struggles. But you shouldn't worry yourself. You did a horrible thing and you're trying hard not to show your confusion. Think of what you did, all the hurt you created. You followed the progression in aggression that led to the death of an old friend. Now, think of the pain the family is going through. You've taken their boy. Your immoral action expressed by your selfish thought of being a man, which turned out to be wrong. Now you will have a journey to carry his memory, as well as yours.

"Take this time as a second chance to mature, to progress in a positive way. You will never forget what you did, but will do your best to better yourself. Since you've taken a life, you must help in bettering people's lives, taking care of the needs of others. To grow as an understanding person, one must learn to balance and appreciate life while helping others. Life has become hard for you because of your actions, but you will learn much as you continue on. Time is what you do have, use it wisely, and be patient. You will learn to be the real person you once were again. You will smile as you sincerely help others."

Walking Down Mitchell Street

Michael Muscadine
Communities United for Restorative Youth Justice

The neighborhood I grew up on is no longer the same. I remember everything about it and how fun it was to live there as a kid. I still have family there to this day and presently live only three blocks away from my grandparents' house. My family moved to Oakland, California, in 1962 and still lives on Mitchell Street. I see a lot of differences with respect to how the community has changed; especially the families and people who stay there now compared to when I was a kid. We all know that neighborhoods change as we get older, some for the better or worse. There are many reasons as to why my neighborhood is not the same anymore.

I remember waking up and always hearing the next-door neighbor's roosters crowing in the morning. It was a nice memory of that "good morning feeling" of waking up to a breakfast in my grandparents' kitchen. Today, there are no more roosters crowing in the hood, not just because some of the families have moved out, but because of something else. The new people moving in call animal services on people with chickens, register complaints on families with dogs that bark; the very sounds that used to give the neighborhood mornings a sense of flavor, if you ask me.

I had a blast as a kid growing up on Mitchell Street, playing football and baseball in the middle of the street with other

kids from around the neighborhood. We made the environment work, running around the neighborhood creeks, building
club houses in the creeks, having water gun and rock wars,
playing hide and seek, riding bikes up and down the street
with friends; the streets were full of kids having fun. These
were the good old days. Now, when I go back to my Gramps
house, I could stay outside for hours kicking back on the porch
with my family or homies, and would not see a kid in sight
playing or riding a bike. I feel like these kids are way too into
video games. Sadly, perhaps it is that parents nowadays are too
scared to let their kids out to play and be outdoors with friends
because of the violence they see on the news every day.

Every city has its problems, especially those without recre-
ational, educational and sports programs for youth. We had one
in the Fruitvale community when I was younger that helped us
stay out of trouble. I don't even see the ice cream trucks of my
youth in the hood. There was an older Mexican man that came
at 5 pm every day to our street. He played a funny horn to let
all the people know he had arrived. He not only had ice cream,
but all the Mexican candy you enjoyed as a kid. The old man's
horn left in me the lifetime memory of kids running outside
with their mom's and dad's, and me and my brothers running
to ask my gramps for a dollar or two. These days, the City of
Oakland makes it hard for ice cream trucks and street vendors
to run these small businesses, working-class people just trying
to make a living. The city is now ticketing poor folks that are
selling goods or trying to make an honest living out here or
make an extra buck to support their families.

I remember as a youth walking up and down Mitchell
Street unafraid. Everyone knew us and even though we got
into some trouble now and then as teens and some of the
neighbors looked at us as crazy, they also said hello. It was
commonplace for families having a party to invite us to come

get something to eat or drink; we always gave them respect. It seemed all of the neighbors knew one another, looked out for each other's homes and property. The best time was the summertime; opening up the fire hydrant on a really hot day to get wet and cool down. Some might say we were wasting water but to me, we were making a hot day go by fast and bringing a whole neighborhood together; the young, adults, even the elderly ladies coming out with buckets to water their gardens. When I was young it seemed like there was a party every other day or just a few guys hanging out playing some Vicente Fernández or Ramón Ayala after a long day of work with a few beers. Now, I feel like these new folks that are moving in are losing that sense of community and of being a neighbor.

Gentrification has stolen this community's spirit and character. New residents like hipsters walk right past you and won't say a thing. They make no effort to meet or get to know long-standing residents and extended families. My familia is one of the last Chicano families that still live in the hood and it feels like I am getting pushed out my own neighborhood. The Oakland Police Department has become very hostile towards the community, especially the Latino and black youth in Fruitvale. New restrictive laws such as Gang Injunctions give police a green light to harass and target Latino families and youth. Stop And Frisk has replaced "Meet and Greet" in Oakland. I no longer feel welcome or like I am part of my own community at times. I am outraged they came up with these bullshit-ass laws. Unprecedented numbers of young people are failing or getting kicked out of school and going to jail, CYA, or ending up in prison. How is it that it becomes acceptable for the government to mistreat and discriminate against our people who are born and raised as Oaklanders? Longtime residents no longer feel safe.

Gentrification worsens daily. Houses are being bought up to raise property values, rents are skyrocketing, driving the working-class family out of the neighborhood. They are forced to move to the suburbs and rural valleys where there is no work or livable wage jobs. Don't get me wrong, there are a lot of families still here but these are the ones that have been here since the 1940s and 1950s who own their homes. Fruitvale still has Latino history and culture. When I was younger I was always happy to go down to East 14th Street and Fruitvale for the Cinco de Mayo festival or Día de los Muertos festival every year. All Raza came out to celebrate culture, share community and have some good food to enjoy. The festivals are not that big anymore and it certainly feels like all we are losing that Oakland Chicano culture.

I really don't go to the festivals anymore because I am a defendant on the Fruitvale Gang Injunction and feel like all eyes are on me when I go to the city. Cops make me feel like I am not part of the community that my family has been a part of for a generation. My home now makes me feel like an outcast. The injunction makes it so I can't even walk down the street and greet a few homeboys I've known since childhood without worrying about these young cops harassing or stopping us for no reason.

I know Oakland has its ups and downs just like every inner city does, but when I'm walking down the street less worried about the gangs, drug dealers and pimps than I am about these rookie cops with itchy trigger fingers, something has gone wrong in my city and this country. Even though my neighborhood is not the same as when I was kid, it's still my hood. I am going to be part of it and make it a better place, giving something back to my people who are still here living. I am working to beautify the community with Chicano murals and helping to guide and support the healthy development of our youngsters. I take walks just reminiscing on all the family that has lived here, through the good, bad and ugly times. Mitchell Street is home and will always be home to me no matter what. Oakland is and always will stay home. I can never forget where I'm from. Now today is Sunday, about to spend time with familia on Mitchell Street and barbecue it up en mi barrio.

A Badge Is Not Impunity

Rubén Leal
Communities United for Restorative Youth Justice

When I was a little kid I always wanted to be a cop. In movies and in the media, they're always portrayed as the good guys. They have guns, catch the bad guys and save the day— you know, "heroes." At block parties, McGruff the Crime-Fighting Dog would come take pictures with us and tell us to "Take a Bite Out of Crime." During Cinco de Mayo, the police used to bring out this cool lowrider (still do) and hit the switches for all the kids. You can understand why a five-year-old would look up to a policeman and want to be one. In 1994, when I was six years old, I got a rude awakening; I witnessed and saw the true colors of these folks who are supposed to be protecting our communities.

One evening my older brother Max, a couple neighborhood friends and I were riding our bikes in front of our house when two officers approached us and immediately ordered us off our bikes. My brother Max got off his bike and started walking it to our house. That's when one of the black officers rushed him, grabbed him by the neck and started choking him, yelling, "Spit it out!" He then slammed him against the Centro Infantil de La Raza's chain-link fence by his neck, continuing to yell, "Spit it out!!!" I saw my brother turning blue from not being able to breathe.

At that moment I dropped my bike and ran inside my house to tell my mom and everyone that the policeman was choking my brother. We all ran out and, when we got outside, this officer was still choking my brother against the chain-link fence. That's when my mother (the captain of the neighborhood watch at the time) and my older brother Chuy started yelling at the cop to stop. He finally stopped choking him, slammed him on the ground, put his knees on my brother's back, handcuffed him and placed him in the back seat of his police car. Apparently the cop said he saw him put something in his mouth, which he believed to be rock cocaine. I remember after they let him go, the cop told my mom he saw him put something in his mouth and he had gotten in eight shootouts in the streets, so that's why he did what he did to my brother. I remember my mom wanted them to take him to the hospital so they could pump his stomach to see if they could find the drugs he had allegedly swallowed.

That was the first time I witnessed police brutality and saw how brutal the Oakland Police Department can be against its civilians and children. My brother was just a kid and had to be only about twelve years old when a policeman nearly choked him to death in front of my home. We filed a complaint and went to city hall to some kind of panel with city officials and they had the cop there. I told them what I witnessed. The city council then told us that they were sorry for what happened to my brother and that he was in the wrong place at the wrong time. Wrong place at the wrong time? In front of our house, playing on our bikes?

Nothing happened to the officers. No disciplinary actions, no training, nothing. That's when I realized at that young age that the cops and OPD are not here to protect us; they are here to enforce and terrorize our communities. They can get away with anything and not be held accountable. I'm not biased against the police; I have seen firsthand and have been a victim of their brutality.

Now as an adult, I have seen numerous OPD officers murder unarmed civilians in cold blood with the same excuse:

"He reached for his waistband."

"I feared for my life."

"I thought he had a gun."

"I thought he swallowed some drugs."

The same old washed-up lines and bam, nothing happens to them. Even Latinos themselves are guilty of police injustice. How does a police officer like Hector Jiménez kill two unarmed civilians—Andrew Moppin and Jody Woodfox (shot in the back while running away)—in less than a year and is still out patrolling the streets? It is time these cops are held accountable for their actions. Every year the City of Oakland and taxpayers pay off millions of dollars in settlements because of OPD misconduct. The city should start taking all of that money out of their fuckin' pensions and see if they continue to beat the shit out of folks on a daily basis. Having a badge does not give them the right to kill with impunity!

To All My Young Brothers

Juan Martínez
Santa Cruz Barrios Unidos Prison Project

To all my young brothers:

First of all, thank you for the opportunity in allowing me to enter your space and talk with you. Please allow me to introduce myself. My name is Juan, and my credentials for writing this letter are simply lots of caring and concern for all my young brothers who are facing hard times ahead. I hope this letter can provide you with something to think about and help you make good choices in the journey you are about to embark upon. And I can't think of no better way than to share with you what I've learned and experienced within my own personal journey behind these walls.

When I first entered the system twenty-three years ago, I was a nineteen-year-old gangbanger with a twenty-nine years to life sentence. My journey, like many of the homies my age, began in a maximum-security level 4 prison. One thing I did, right away, unlike many of the homies my age, was to get involved by signing up to the library to begin checking out books on philosophy, social and political criticism, psychology, sociology, world mythology and many other subjects. I remember in school teachers telling me I was gifted in learning things, so I figured, "Since I'm going to be in prison, might as well learn something useful." Unbeknownst to me at the time was how significant this learning would become throughout my journey. Let me share with you an experience I had while I was still housed in a maximum security that changed the trajectory of my journey, and continues to set the tone for me on how to navigate these perilous waters. It had the power to transform me to be the man I am today.

As I mentioned, I have been an avid reader. One day a big brother (I call him "a gift in disguise") called me over and asked me, "Hey, I always see you reading. What are you reading?" So I showed him the book. Then he told me something I'll never forget. He said, "You know, you're not like others (meaning the other homies there). There's something about you. I've been watching you and you're always reading. So let me give you some advice: Never raise your hand to volunteer for anything. Continue minding your own businesses. And ALWAYS, ALWAYS listen to your heart because, if it is not in your heart, don't get involved with the prison politics and violence. Don't be afraid to say no to that lifestyle, because saying no to that lifestyle is not going to make you be any less of a man!! Just keep it real!!"

I was young at the time, and like any young man from the gang lifestyle, I thought of myself as this crazy ass chingón, down for my neighborhood, willing to prove myself for the homies, but this big brother was telling me to listen to my heart. I remember asking myself, "What the fuck is he talking about?" I guess he could see the expression on my face because he asked me, "When you are alone at night, away from the noise and all the crazy shit, who are the people you think of the most? Do you miss your family? Who are the people you miss?" I had to be honest with myself, and the truth was I did miss my family. He then asked me, "Are you willing to put your family second? Because if you are, then they are not that important to you. So, are you willing to sacrifice your family and return for the prison life and violence?" My response was that family is the most important part of my life and that I was not willing to sacrifice them because nothing matters more. Big brother then shared some life changing words, "Well then, this is a good thing. It means that prison politics and the violence is not for you."

Thanks to this voice of reason, I can now see how significant it is that I have realized this truth in my heart. You see, most men in prison who are involved in the prison politics and violence don't make it through. That's because their heart was never in it to begin with. This is because they've never looked inside and listened to their heart, because if they would have done so, they would've seen and realized they were never willing to sacrifice their families and themselves for this lifestyle, and were simply acting for self-recognition, out of fear and peer pressure, only being used as sacrificial pawns for someone else's false cause.

You know something, my young brothers? I am very thankful that fate allowed me to cross paths with this big brother— a truly rare gift! So when you begin your journey, my young brothers, ask yourself what is in your heart and truly listen to it, and don't be afraid to speak what's truly in your heart because people will respect you. Although some may criticize you for it, underneath, in the quietness of their hearts, they are actually praising you because nothing gains more respect in here than a man who truly knows himself, and talks the talk and walks the walk.

Also, stay away from those who are rowdy and boisterous, who tell stories of shit they say they've done when in reality they just create that shit in their heads—half-truths and half lies! Putting themselves as they are telling their fake stories in the middle of the story seeking the spotlight. Stay away from these guys, who are many. They can be dangerous because they are seeking to build their own reputation and want desperately to be known. And in their stupidity, they are willing to do anything and can easily sweep you along with them. Another way you'll recognize this group, besides being rowdy and boisterous, is because they like to express their opinions about everything that is going on in prison, and are always involved in other peoples' business. In fact, these are the kind that eventually end up as "pawns" in someone else's cause. So be careful not to seek self-recognition and a reputation based on false values of manhood, importance and power, because it is a dangerous path.

Also, stay away from drugs and all those who are involved with drugs. I cannot emphasize this enough. I've seen so many camaradas that were on the right path, begin using drugs or become involved with drugs, and now it is heartbreaking watching them without their dignity and self-worth. So be careful and stay away from these groups.

So my young brothers, whether your journey is a long journey or a short one, my heart and goodwill will always be focused on you. Remember to always listen to your heart. Also, cultivate your mind, because it is the greatest and only weapon you'll ever need. Educate yourself by creating the habit of reading and studying. Guard what you have learned and all the knowledge you have received. I have learned that knowledge is a precious commodity and has value, but it has to be balanced out with self-control. I've seen a lot of very "smart" homies who are also emotionally unstable. When this happens, what you end up with is a very smart but undisciplined "foolish" homie. So constantly question and evaluate yourself about seeking self-recognition and pride rooted in lies, because it is a very powerful desire and many fall into it only to find emptiness and regret.

Finally, seek a spiritual path whatever your beliefs may be. However, don't use spirituality as a "crutch" simply to relieve momentary feelings of emptiness or disillusionment; this can also be another trap that many fall into. Spirituality is sacred, and it demands respect and reverence. If you seek it humbly, in the quietness of your heart, not only will it guide you in the right path, but it will also help you discover more about your true self. More importantly, it has the power to transform you, giving you courage based on truth. Unfortunately, many use spirituality momentarily as a crutch, and hide behind spiritu-ality when things are challenging, only to go back to their old selves once difficult challenges pass away. Even worse, there are many who hide their defects in secret behind some form of organized religion (spirituality and religion are two distinct subjects in my view). Instead, face the challenges you face in life with dignity and integrity, exploring and overcoming weakness, walking true.

So, my young brothers, remember that it is not about the destination, it is about the journey! It is about the series of steps and events continuously unfolding as you make your way through life. I honor the words given to me by our big brother who set me on the right path. Not only his words of wisdom, but also many others like him inside and outside prison who have been instrumental in helping me be the man I am today. Remember also that you are not alone, and as long as you stay in the shade (stay low), believe me that those who know the way, will come to offer guidance as you walk along your journey.

A humble servant,
Juan

Message to My Seventeen-Year-Old Self

Roberto Martínez
Santa Cruz Barrios Unidos Prison Project
California Conservation Corps
Susanville Level III

First and foremost allow me to extend my utmost love and respect to you in full strives.

As I sit behind these walls and think about what I could've done differently, I would tell the seventeen-year-old young me to love life and not take it for granted. At any given time it could be taken away from you, in the blink of an eye. I would also tell the seventeen-year-old me to learn from the mistakes my elders made. I would have given more time to my familia, giving my two little boys the love and attention and guidance they needed. I would have also treated my kids' mother with more respect.

I would have taken school more seriously and strived to better serve mi Raza by how I lived. By this I mean involving myself in things that made my community stronger instead of giving my people a bad name. I would stop giving the world a valid reason to look down upon us Chicanos from the barrio. I would've listened to my dad and older homeboys when they told me there's nothing good that comes out of gangs and street life besides death and prison.

I would also stop being selfish. We are being selfish when we hurt the people we love, most of all, our familia. Too many homeboys who have kids are leaving them behind to fend for themselves, to fall victim to the streets that have love for no one. We leave our kids looking for a father who should have given them the love and instruction they need to grow up right and become good people. Instead, I'm sitting in a California State Prison doing nine years at the age of eighteen.

I have now seen my first prison and all I can say is I should have stayed home that one night that changed my life forever. Prison ain't anything like the thug life lies romanticize it to be; it doesn't make you a man or a real gangsta. All it is, is a lot of locked up grown men who wish they could just get one more chance in life. I walk the yard with a homeboy of mine; his prison sentence is fifty-eight years to life, which means he has to do his full fifty-eight years before the board sees him. He tells me all the time there is no chance he will ever go home. Once you're locked up, everyone forgets about you; it's like you fell off the face of the earth. All I can tell you brothers and sisters is to focus on your education; become something more than a prison member or a body count to the homicide rate.

In prison there's those who still front or think they're pimps, ballers and rappers: we call them wishers. Then you have some who are still trying to make a name for themselves. All together, the notion that prison is a badge of honor is full of shit. Prison is nothing but a waste of life and time. You are a modern-day slave wasting away rather than being changed towards the kind of person who is contributing something to the world. All I can say is, think before you do. Don't let no one make you do something you don't want to do. Don't swallow the thug life and baller lies, but find the true meaning of being Chicano. I'll keep you in my prayers.

Love & respect,
Your Brother in the Struggle

Raza Cósmica: Barrio and Pinto Arte,
Community Mural Projects and
Cultura Tattoo Arts

"Untitled," Michael Roybal
Submitted by CURYJ, Michael
Muscadine

"Máscaras y lágrimas," Frank de Jesús Acosta

"Marisol" (the artist's sister), Alberto Symon, a.k.a. Beto
Paint and pencil
Submitted by CURYJ, Michael Muscadine

"Root of All Evil," Alberto
Symon, a.k.a. Beto
Pencil and paint on paper
Submitted by CURYJ,
Michael Muscadine

"Spill the Wine," Sal Cortez, Jr., a.k.a. Chamuco
Drawing/Tattoo Art
Submitted by CURYJ, Michael Muscadine

"Chicano through the Decades," Sal Cortez, Jr., a.k.a. Chamuco
Painting on canvas (5 pieces)
Submitted by CURYJ, Michael Muscadine

"ESO" (East Side Oakland), Sal Cortez, Jr., a.k.a. Chamuco
Drawing/Tattoo Art
Submitted by CURYJ, Michael Muscadine

"Sitting in the Park," Sal Cortez, Jr., a.k.a. Chamuco
Painting
Submitted by CURYJ, Michael Muscadine

"RIP Mitchell St. Joke," Sal
    Cortez, Jr., a.k.a. Chamuco
Drawing
Submitted by CURYJ, Michael
    Muscadine

"Untitled 1," Sergio A. Rangel
Drawing
Submitted by Michael
    Muscadine, CURYJ

"Untitled 2," Sergio A. Rangel
Drawing
Submitted by CURYJ, Michael Muscadine

"Untitled 3," Sergio A. Rangel
Drawing
Submitted by CURYJ, Michael
    Muscadine

"Stop the Violence," Rene Enriquez
Drawing
Submitted by Barrios Unidos

"Huelga," Garcia

"Unititled 1," Frankie Alejandrez
Drawing
Submitted by Barrios Unidos

"Unititled 2," Frankie Alejandrez

"Untitled 3," Frankie
Alejandrez

"Untitled 4," Frankie
Alejandrez

Communities United for Restorative Youth Justice
CURYJ

The (CURYJ) Mural Project is a core strategy for cultural expression, education, building community, organizing, advocacy and promoting ownership for neighborhood beautification in Oakland, California, and surrounding areas. Mural art has long been a widely utilized medium for lifting up voices of dissent within oppressed communities and in pan-Latino liberation movements. Inter-generational pan-Latino organizers, activists and artists continue this tradition of social expression and change activism.

Mural on 27th street, CURYJ. Submitted José Luis Pavón.

Building Community from the Ground Up/Fruitvale Community Garden,
Dime, Peps357. Drama, Xochitl Guerrero, Alberto Symon.
The garden was started organically, grassroots style "from the ground up,"
hence the name and message of the mural, "Building Community from the
Ground Up." It was produced by a group of lifelong residents, neighbors,
friends and organizers involved in the Stop the Injunctions Coalition. They
envisioned that an empty lot overgrown with weeds could be an asset rather
than an eyesore; all it needed was some attention, some hands-on work,
some plants and dedicated people to turn it into the beautiful space it is
today.

As the Fruitvale garden demonstrates, strong communities grow beautiful
things from the ground up. Land is a community resource and an important
element in stability such as stable housing and community space. CURYJ
believes that the people who live in a city should have access to city land.
They also believe that indigenous land is for people to thrive on, not to be
fenced in or sold. The garden is maintained as a spot for community-
building, a green space for healthy food production, a gathering place for
cultural traditions and for art. The vision of this garden builds on
momentum built by the Stop the Injunctions Coalition and the Aztlán
Beautification Movement to move our community towards short-term and
long-term solutions for safety, health and well-being.

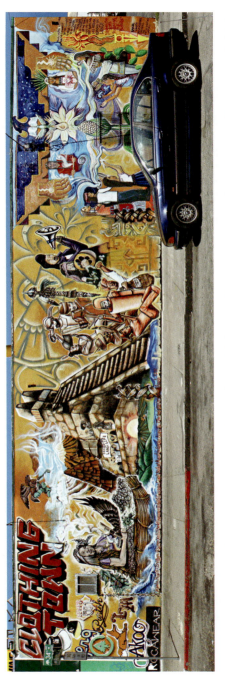

Growing Our Roots, Reclaiming Our Fruitvale, Dime, Peps357. Drama, Xochitl Guerrero, Alberto Symon. Property of CURYJ. This mural was a community response to the implementation of the Fruitvale gang injunction in Oakland, California. In partnership with defendants of the gang injunction, the Fruitvale community, Stop the Injunctions Coalition, Xicana Moratorium Coalition, East Side Arts Alliance and Aztlán Beautification Movement completed this work.

Barrio Unity, Drama, Dime1, Peps357. Submitted by Rubén Leal, Property of CURYJ.

The overall message of this piece is to promote small neighborhood businesses, cultural and community "hood" unity. It is a collaborative project between the Aztlán Beautification Movement and Visual Element.

Community, Safety and Peace, 2011.

Paso Robles Mural Project:
"Community, Safety and Peace"

Frank de Jesús Acosta

In early 2011, building on recent public art projects involving youth and teens in the California Central Coast community of Paso Robles, artist and author Henry A. J. Ramos of Studios on the Park partnered with then-Paso Robles Police Chief Lisa Solomon and Mary Legleiter, an art teacher at Paso Robles High School, to support a youth-driven mural project called "Community, Safety and Peace."

Chief Solomon provided grant support for the effort through the Police Activities League, and more than twenty local youth, ages sixteen to twenty-one, most of them at-risk Latino boys and men, participated in the project's design and implementation.

Ramos had led a similar effort during his own youth in Los Angeles during the late 1970s. He had thus seen firsthand the power of creative expression and mural-making as a ready means of mobilizing young people to meaningful action on the issues most relevant to them.

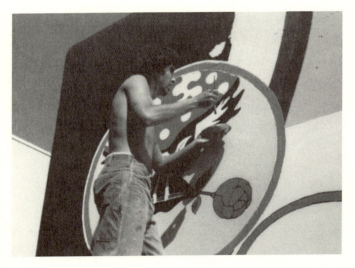

Artist and author Henry A. J. Ramos, age 17, "War & Peace" mural, Los Angeles, 1977.

An inspiration for the Paso Robles project had been the recent pre-dating, and still-unsolved death of one of Ramos' youth art workers following the young man's twenty-first birthday celebration at a local bar. The youth's body was found on the train tracks the next morning; and various friends and peers who had been with him the night of his death suggested that gang conflict had likely been involved as a precipitating factor. The mural project's focus on issues of "Community, Safety and Peace" was intended as a direct response to these unhappy circumstances; and the project had a discernible unifying effect on the entire community. *The Paso Robles Press*, the area's leading newspaper, ran a cover story on the project in its Community Section on February 11, 2011; and on April 19, 2011 the Paso Robles City Council presented participating youth with a formal commendation. The original work is now featured prominently as a permanent fixture at the entrance of Paso Robles' main downtown library.

Latino youth artist designing mural at Studios on the Park, Paso Robles, CA.

Key participants and creative drivers in this work included local Mexican-American youth Mason López, Salvador Chávez, Abisal Ortiz, "Braurio," Pablo Estrada, Edgar Jiménez, Jorge López and Saúl Sepúlveda.

Each of these young men were or had been students at Paso Robles High School. Several were on their way to graduation, but all were at risk of falling through the cracks or otherwise being lost, whether at school, at home or in the local criminal justice system.

Mason López, then age nineteen and one of the project leaders, had been struggling with Attention Deficit Disorder (ADD) and drug abuse. His efforts to make things right by joining the U.S. Navy had been foiled when armed forces recruiters informed him the Navy could not admit him owing to his ADD condition and allied issues. He struggled with homelessness and anger. Art became a refuge for him. The project brought forward his remarkable talent as a visual artist and his innate leadership skills, resulting in Ramos designating him as one of the project's two principal youth co-leaders.

Abisal Ortiz, mural designing, Studios on the Park, Paso Robles, 2011.

Abisal Ortiz and Salvador Chávez also emerged as partic-ularly gifted artists in the course of their participation on the mural project. Each contributed important design elements to the final product.

Paso Robles High School art instructor Mary Legleiter had taught some of the participating youth in her classes at the high school. But she often reflected throughout the produc-tion of the "Community, Safety and Peace" mural that many Latino youth in the community's schools—and especially young Latino men and boys—were hard-pressed to excel at and complete their studies owing to the economic and politi-cal pressures of the day affecting their lives and families. Many simply tracked with remedial education classes. Many ended up not graduating.

When the project culminated at a standing-room-only Paso Robles City Council meeting to commemorate the youth-led effort and dedicate the final product to the town's

Salvador Chávez, youth artist at Studios on the Park, Paso Robles, CA, 2011.

High School art instructor Mary Legleiter and youth artists, Studios on the Park, Paso Robles, CA, 2011.

main library for permanent display, parents of these young men approached the supervising artist, Henry Ramos to express their gratitude. Their pride and joy were unmistakenly evident. Many were in tears. In the course of these exchanges, Ramos confirmed that virtually none of the Latino youth artist's parents (most of them undocumented immigrants or noncitizens with permanent resident status) had ever before attended a city council meeting. It was the closest to American democracy and civic process they had ever been.

Communities all across the State of California and the nation would benefit from greater public and community support for constructive, youth-driven public art projects like "Community, Safety and Peace." The project served to promote community healing in a time of tension resulting from the recent apparent gang-related killing of a young man. It brought together an active cohort of talented youth from the community, who learned they could be galvanized and heard

"Community, Safety and Peace" Mural in progress, Studios on the Park, Paso Robles, CA, 2011.

through artistic expression. It engaged local police, civic leaders and allied institutions and helped them to see these youth through a more affirmative and constructive lens. And it helped several of the participating youth to pursue additional creative studies and employment, building on their positive experience in this work.

One wonders why more public and private investment in projects of this sort are so difficult to find these days, particularly when their beneficial impacts are so significant and manifest.

My Cultural Path to Healing
Tomás Alejo

My name is Tomás Alejo and I was born in Watsonville, a small agricultural community on the central coast of California with a long history of labor and social justice struggles. Our family story was a migrant experience, following the harvest from California to places like Weslaco in the Rio Grande Valley of Texas, literally one of the poorest communities in the United States. We lived and worked for five years there. At the age of thirteen, the family moved back to Watsonville, where for the next seven years I would build a dubious history of trouble with the law, addiction, alcoholism, drug rehab and incarceration.

My first experience with drug court, rehab and juvenile hall was when I was sixteen years old; the probation officer told me I was the worst case of alcohol and drug addiction he had seen for someone my age. Despite several stints in conventional rehabilitation programs, even my first exposure to a highly successful culturally based program, Sí Se Puede, I continued my cycle of substance abuse, legal trouble, rehab, relapse and incarceration. Upon turning eighteen years old, I was facing a serious case when the judge gave me the option of joining the military in lieu of incarceration in an adult prison. After an uncle sicked a military recruiter on me, I joined the National Guard, who had negotiated this alternate sentencing with the judge (i.e., this type of sentencing was actually a common practice by judges before two decades of Three Strikes and mandatory punishment laws took root).

It saddens me, however, to confess that, being me, the National Guard kept me local enough to continue my return to my same old stomping grounds and old habits. My drug addiction got worse and eventually landed me in prison. By the time I was twenty years old, I had literally done time in every juvenile hall, every jail and adult penitentiary from San Francisco to Salinas, including Kern State Prison, Delano C.C.C., Soledad and San Quentin. If there is any saving grace to this time incarcerated, it is that I took my first steps to healing and reform by getting involved in movimiento political learning circles in prison. The reality is that inmates are forced to join or belong to one group or another just out of shear survival. I too joined out of instinct for these reasons.

Although I joined a literary circle out of a sense of survival, I lucked out to land in this group which pushed for education as a vehicle for rehabilitation and advancement. People don't realize that in prison, the influence of Chicanismo and/or Cultura-based identity plays out not always in the most positive ways, such as when employed as an organizing tool for survival, violence and power on the inside. Despite this negative iteration of desperation, Cultura often asserts its own power and heals, moving men towards positive identity, rehabilitation and a path to changing their lives while on the inside and upon release. I witnessed this happen to me and many others. The group I joined happened to have a literary circle. This experience introduced me to classical literature, for which I found I had great natural comprehension. This realization of innate intelligence flew in the face of what had been drilled into my head in school and other places along my path. I applied this acumen to a thirst for learning, including Chicano history and culture, and a broader multi-cultural understanding. I fed my mind and soul poetry, literature, especially inter-cultural voices of social and political historical dissent.

This early path to wholeness was marked by many false starts. I had made my mind up to do whatever it took to pursue a higher education upon release from prison. I actually did enroll in community college, but dropped off because of returning to the lifestyle, relapse and attendant parole violation and recidivism. Growing up, my family members were staunch supporters of César Chávez and the United Farm Workers, participating in many actions, demonstrations and marches throughout my childhood and adult life. My own awakening of political consciousness and identity had led me to working with a few other brothers in the community to organize learning circles out in the community with young ones in danger of following our path and bad example.

During this time I dabbled in two worlds. In this period of light and dark, my forays into community organizing and youth service allowed me to meet several people who would become mentors, spiritual teachers, healers and elders. Gang and street violence had risen dramatically in Chicano, Latino and other communities of color and was taking young lives in unprecedented numbers. Violence had become the number one cause of death for our young by the mid-to-late 1990s. At a local community peace conference and gang summit in 1995, I met two people who became most influential in my life: "Nane" Alejandrez and Albino García of Santa Cruz Barrios Unidos. These two individuals and the circle of relations within which they did their groundbreaking peace work would expose me to the missing element to standing sobriety and a path of purpose: La Cultura Cura. Since our meeting, and throughout my bumpy journey to the present, Albino García remained a mentor, teacher and spiritual guide.

Much like many impoverished Latino communities, Watsonville has many of the attendant pitfalls of street violence, gangs, substance abuse and the illegal drug economy. My life work would be dedicated to changing this reality. In my educational path, I developed a passion for reading and was able to expand my consciousness regarding political and life-altering understanding of cultural expression. While still being locked up, I studied the philosophical writings of Carl Jung, Alan Watts, J. Krishnamurti, Ram Das, Frantz Fanon and George Jackson, among others. With love and support from my family and community, I would finally be able to break away from destructive patterns and enroll in school, excelling in academia after being released. This was not a simple journey, but rather a serpentine road of hits and misses, substance abuse relapses and parole violations.

Prior to being released from my very last term of incarceration, I began following the cultural, spiritual, ceremonial practices of my ancestors. These became the centerpiece of my own healing and sobriety, as well as my philosophical framework for service in the community. While returning to school, I continued to participate and organize healing and teaching circles with the Brown Berets in Watsonville. I was mentored by Albino and immersed myself in the teachings of Maestro Jerry Tello and his Joven/Hombre Noble Círculo Curriculum. I began attending the ceremonial Sundance at Camp McDermott and became a Dancer in 2012. La Cultura Cura became the connection between my own personal healing and helping to heal the inter-generational trauma of my family and community.

In 2010, I was awarded a Bachelor's Degree in Sociology from the University of California, Santa Cruz with an emphasis on race inequity and prisoner justice and was awarded the J. Herman Blake Award for community service. In 2013, I completed a Masters in Social Work from San Jose State University with an emphasis in Mental Health. I have since served, interned and volunteered in many community groups, non-profit agencies and grassroots political organizations. Currently, I am serving as a program director at Identity Inc., a nonprofit social service organization in Montgomery County, Maryland. As part of my broader commitment to the Movimiento bringing healing wholeness back to our communities, I have worked with Maestro Jerry Tello, Albino García, Luis Cardona and others to bring the Joven/Hombre Noble and La Cultura Cura model to Washington DC and the East Coast. The cultural mix of the pan-Latino populations (e.g., Salvadoran, Guatemalan, Nicaraguan, Dominican, Puerto Rican, Caribbean and South American) will lend to many wonderful revelations and innovations in the evolution of our La Cultura Cura model which has been explored largely on the West Coast.

During my seven-year sojourn in the darkness of incarceration, I was blessed to discover, and began to nurture, the vision and skill of creating cultural tattoo art. It began as a simple way of gaining acceptance, of maintaining relationships with people on the outside and as a way to make some money while incarcerated. While tattooing had some very practical benefits as a marketable skill, such as making me feel self-reliant and autonomous as a prisoner, it quickly became a vehicle for healing, expression and discovery of identity. It was an instrument of learning, cultural understanding and exchange, a way of creating bonds and community. As a tool of survival in prison, it provided a symbol of freedom and defiance from the dehumanization that occurs on the inside of the jailhouse, detention center and prison walls.

The more I delved in and mastered the art form, the more I came to see tattooing as having a much deeper place in cultural healing and expression. It is important to understand the place that tattooing has as a cultural art form and practice for many oppressed people, a way of preserving our history of struggle against colonial hegemony. Many of our ancestors, elders and contemporary peers have known the pain of having our cultures forcibly and insidiously purged. The art form has been a cultural pathway to recovery and the preserving our history, iconography and spiritual traditions. Tattooing is a very personal art form that represents expression of historical memory, cultural and spiritual sovereignty. In Western society it is in many ways a distinctively defiant art form, a symbol of counterculture. Isn't it ironic that tattooing is illegal in prison? You can be charged with destruction of private property if caught giving or receiving a tattoo as an inmate. Or is it telling of what people are really regarding in a capitalist society?

Tattooing is a revered cultural practice in many indigenous societies. In some Polynesian cultures, tattoos are ways of asserting identity of clan, a badge of honor for deeds and accomplishments, and some special status bestowed upon someone. Also, Polynesians incorporate the tattoo as a symbol of rites of passage from childhood to adulthood, of lessons learned, life-affirming milestones accomplished and deeds of honor. Many cultures use tattoos as part of a spiritual ceremony and expression. Across cultures the use and place of tattoos as personal expressions of identity and culture are evident. This is certainly true for Chicanos and pan-Latinos of indigenous descent.

As a tattoo artist myself, I incorporate into my own walk these cultural principles of teaching, healing and renewal of identity, communal belonging, preservation and transformation. Many tattoo artists across cultures keep it sacred in this way, not as fashion or fad. For example, when I draw blood from someone during tattooing, it is a responsibility, something sacred and spiritual. Those I work with understand this as ceremony in many ways. We bless the work area to invite the spirit and focus on the meaning of the symbol or artwork, the relationship it has to the person's cultural and spiritual journey, and the statement of commitment or revelation it makes. We share stories of pain, healing, victory, noble purpose and destiny. We speak of dreams for our communities and ourselves. It is at once therapy and medicine. This puts tattooing in its proper place in our communities and society. The ritual and resultant art is our truth, the reaffirming of our redemptive being, healing, reconciliation, restoring, reclaiming, culture, history, identity and purpose; love among us, between us and the Creator.

Tomás Alejo's Tattoo Art

Tonatiuh Huitzilopochtli, known to the Aztecs as the Fifth Sun, El Quinto Sol and leader of the heavens.

La Calavera, the sugar skull representing those ancestors who have moved on to the spirit world and transformation.

La Adelita, the female revolutionary soldier of Mexico.

Quetzalcoatl Xolotl, the Aztec deity Quetzalcoatl eating the heart of knowledge and wisdom.

Nahui Ollin, four movements, the earthquake. Nothing is static; everything is in constant motion. What appears solid is flowing energy.

Coatlicue Tonantzin, Sacred Earth Mother, she who gives life to all things.

La Luna, the feminine energy, the giver of life.

Huitzil, the hummingbird, representation of Quetzalcoatl.

Huehueteotl, the old god of fire, wisdom and knowledge.

Calaca, transformation, the cycle of life and death.

Celtic Dragon, flying with water symbols: the amalgamation of cultures and power.

Nahui Ollin II, four movements, the earthquake. Nothing is static; everything is in constant motion. What appears solid is flowing energy.

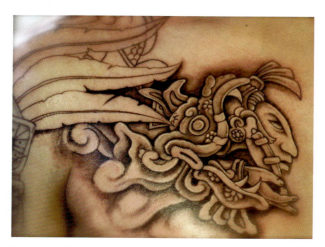

Kukulkan, the Mayan feathered serpent deity of knowledge and rationality.

Conclusion

Frank de Jesús Acosta and Henry A. J. Ramos

Our cultura is the worldview that accounts for us as individuals, families and community; accounts for our dignity, gifts, moral compass and mutual respect as members of the human family; and provides a path of harmony and ecology with all creation.

Our purpose in compiling this book of testimonies and creative expression has been to lift up pathways to health and well-being for at-risk Latino men and boys (LMBs). We have included real life experiences to underscore the human impact of punitive versus restorative pathways from mass incarceration. In so doing, we have featured a collection of carefully curated, first-voice poetry, self-reflections, essays and art by Latino young men and boys who have been engaged and/or are advocating reform in the California criminal and juvenile justice system.

We also featured topical essays by community advocates and practitioners of culturally based practice (e.g., La Cultura Cura) to provide some substantive introductory context on inequities in the justice system and important issues rooted in race-based disparity facing LMBs. A sequel publication will critically examine and lift up criteria for highly successful institutional practices and replicable program strategies to achieve improved health, education and employment outcomes for LMBs, based on field research and leadership testimonials.

An expansive body of research has confirmed what poor communities of color have known and raised their voice in dissent over, long before the civil rights movement began. The disparities created by poverty, institutional racism, discrimination and recalcitrant inequalities are condemning children and youth of color to lifetimes of egregious social, economic and political disenfranchisement. While education is touted as the great equalizer in American society, the failure to provide a quality, equitable and accessible education to poor communities of color sixty years after *Brown vs Board of Education* largely fuels the endangered status of boys and men of color in America.

Boys and men of color in America, certainly those of pan-Latino, Native American and Black descent, face a kind of double jeopardy. They live in a society that rejects, marginalizes and disrespects their cultural heritage; the vestiges of colonization remain strong in "American" society (i.e., hegemony—imposing the dominant culture and punishing them when they rebel). These are continuing forms of racism and discrimination: the imposition of a Euro-centric worldview that breaks down the social fabric and cultural/spiritual traditions, values and rites of passage that take LMBs from healthy childhood development to responsible adulthood. Also, the individualism and decadence-oriented mores, that undergird capitalism and its institutions, are counter-intuitive to the familial, communal and ecologically focused economic values espoused by many of the cultures that compromise this nation's large and growing Latino community.

Simultaneously, children of all races, cultures and creeds are being reared in a mechanized, celluloid and cyber society that breeds alienation, estrangement, growing nihilism, anes-

thetization to violence and human detachment with little
veneration for life or sense of noble purpose. Our 2007 book,
*The History of Barrios Unidos: Healing Community Violence,
Cultura Es Cura*, made the following points to illustrate the
plight of children and young persons of color:

> Each generation's struggle for justice is framed against
> the backdrop of chronic inequality. Thus, perhaps, the
> most accurate bell-weather for the vitality of Ameri-
> can democracy today is the welfare of our children and
> the degree to which poverty and violence permeate
> the fabric of our society. Dr. Robert M. Franklin of the
> Interdenominational Theological Center, speaking
> before an Institute for Community Peace conference
> in 1996, used a passage from Mary Shelley's classic
> novel *Frankenstein* to illustrate metaphorically the
> dimensions of youth violence in our time. The passage
> captures the dramatic highpoint of Shelly's story: Dr.
> Victor Frankenstein coming face to face with the dis-
> gruntled monster he had stitched together from the
> stolen remains of corpses to create a "perfect" human
> specimen. The words uttered by the benighted crea-
> ture to his creator bear a haunting resemblance to the
> mindset and mood of young people today, who in so
> many instances have been abandoned by America's
> increasingly tattered assemblage of adults, communi-
> ties and institutions: "I am malicious because I am mis-
> erable. Am I not shunned and hated by all mankind?
> All around me I see bliss from which I alone am irrev-
> ocably excluded. You, my creator, would tear me to
> pieces. Consider that and tell me why I should pity
> man more than he pities me? If I cannot inspire love, I

will cause fear. I was virtuous, misery made me a fiend. Make me happy, and again I shall be good."

In the process of neglecting and abandoning, then criminalizing and demonizing contemporary youth, we are mass-producing such sentiments among those who are relegated to the far fringes of society. The imaginative use of Mary Shelley's book by Dr. Franklin does not apply solely to poor young people of color. He has also aptly connected the sentiments of Dr. Frankenstein's monster to outbreaks of violence among young people reared in comfortable homes and communities where a profound inner emptiness, alienation and misery often equally reside. According to Dr. Franklin, a growing array of factors account for our society's expanding incidence of youth violence—a general sense among young people of spiritual crisis, a deep aimlessness, a lack of noble purpose and isolation from family and community. These sensibilities, which transcend race, class and culture, speak to a creeping detachment from higher universal values or "moral literacy" and seem to characterize too much of what is happening in our society today.

For Latino boys and young men of indigenous descent, the moral literacy of which Dr. Franklin speaks, is culture or La Cultura Cura, which "teaches enduring virtues—justice, truth, goodness, compassion and magnanimity—that flow from the humanity of all cultures, and that can be distilled from history's most redemptive lessons."

The LMB voices featured in this book come from California, the West Coast and Southwest. Each of our partner organizations works on restorative justice and broader disparity-related issues facing Latino boys and young men. For example, the

National Compadres Network (NCN) has adapted the La Cultura Cura model to more than one hundred communities across the country to tailor and account for the diverse make-up and experiences of the pan-Latino population.

What do the various Latino ethnicities have in common? All have their own culture, spirituality and authentic self, which face healing and recovery from the disequilibrium of forced Western assimilation and acculturation. Race matters, but it is culture and its associated values, virtues and traditions that truly define a person's and group's identity, and that can additionally determine their well-being as individuals, families, communities and members of a pluralistic society. The NCN, Barrios Unidos, CURYJ, Homies Unidos, La Plazita Institute and several of the best-practice groups rooted in La Cultura Cura have developed a framework being embraced nationally as a building block for LBM. The Cultura Cura model is a living, breathing and growing philosophy with values, principles and an evolving framework of culturally rooted strategies that can be embraced in any community setting and applied across the spectrum of social interventions (e.g., restorative justice, violence prevention, gang intervention, alternative education and community development).

In closing, our fundamental aim in writing this book was to bring a more human face and collective spirit of understanding to an important but little understood population group in our culture whose circumstances warrant urgent public attention and response. We wanted in addition, to advocate broad experimentation with and adoption of Restorative Transformative Justice values and strategies by law enforcement practitioners in California and elsewhere across the nation. The featured writings and creative works in this book seek to harness a chorus of voices in support of new ways to think about and act on justice in America; they seek to articulate and promote a more humane, comprehensive public sector and community-based response to crime and violence beyond the present model, which has produced disastrous results for low-income communities of color with virtually no associated evidence of larger societal gain. A restorative or transformative justice model would include rehabilitation, healing, reconciliation and restorative value-based approaches in the administration of justice and the corrections system, including collective efforts supporting rehabilitation and the successful return of LBM to their families and communities via comprehensive re-entry strategies.

The essence of Restorative Justice denotes a society's trust to arbitrate constructive corrective action upon those who have breached laws which must be justly and equitably applied. To be sure, this means holding people accountable for legal offences they have committed (and especially for serious infractions that endanger others or deny them of their legitimate property). In such cases, the appropriate penalty may include a time-specific levy of reasonable physical restrictions or other suspensions of freedoms and/or rights as punishment.

But as part of re-creating a social dialogue that moves America's "moral compass" towards a restorative rather than punitive justice system, we must challenge ourselves as well to view the issues through the lens of higher humanity. The growing dialogue for change in the administration of justice in the United States must challenge us to honestly and critically examine the equality and/or disparity of the present system. If we truly live in a free and democratic society, then we have a special responsibility in this connection to ensure that our system meets the basic litmus test of achieving equality in the administration of justice.

This cannot merely be an academic exercise. There is a moral imperative demanding Americans of all backgrounds to question how our democratic society became the one that incarcerates more people than any other nation in the world, and especially people of color. In the spirit of *In Lak'ech Hala Ken* (the Mayan belief and life principle that, I am the other you and you are the other me), let us embody the moral precept that we are all inter-connected, and that as individuals, families, communities and a society, none of us can truly be whole, unless we are all whole.

Biographies of Contributors and Editors

Frank de Jesús Acosta is principal of Acosta & Associates, a California-based consulting group that specializes in professional support services to public and private social change ventures in the areas of children, youth and family services, violence prevention, community development and cultural fluency. Acosta provides writing and strategic professional support in research, planning, and development to foundations and community-centered institutions on select initiatives focused on advancing social justice, equity and pluralism. In 2007, Acosta published *The History of Barrios Unidos* (Arte Público Press, 2007) and is presently authoring and editing a book series focused on issues related to boys and young men of color for Arte Público Press.

Daniel "Nane" Alejandrez is founder of the national urban peace organization Barrios Unidos and has dedicated much of his adult life to educating and combating gangs, drugs and poverty in Latino communities. Since 1977, Santa Cruz Barrios Unidos (BU) has initiated culturally and spiritually based strategies to reach youth involved in gangs and the cycle of community violence. BU operates the César E. Chávez School for Social Change; BU Productions, a micro-enterprise providing jobs and training; and the Community Technology and Resource Center. Nane has received the Martin Luther King,

Jr. Award and the Sankofa Lifetime Achievement Award for his community peace, social justice and multi-cultural unity work.

Father Gregory Boyle is the founder and executive director of Homeboy Industries, the largest gang intervention, rehabilitation and re-entry program in the United States, now its in twenty-fifth year. Father Greg is the author of *The New York Times* bestselling book, *Tattoos on the Heart: The Power of Boundless Compassion* (Free Press, 2011), which has been honored by the Southern California Indie Booksellers Association, Pen USA, *Publishers Weekly* and Goodreads Choice Awards. Father Greg has received numerous honorary degrees, awards and recognitions, including the Civic Medal of Honor, the California Peace Prize and in 2011 was inducted into the California Hall of Fame.

George Galvis holds a Masters in Community Planning from the University of California-Berkeley and since 1993 has been dedicated to promoting non-violent values and strategies to end violence, restore community and reclaim youth from the madness plaguing our streets. Galvis is co-founder and executive director of Communities United for Restorative Youth Justice, while also serving with the White Bison Well-briety Institute, the Criminal Justice Initiative Panel at Solidago Foundation, Intertribal Friendship House and Youth Together, pioneering culturally and spiritually based approaches to build and strengthen healthy individuals, families and communities.

Luis J. Rodríguez is the Poet Laureate of Los Angeles, chosen by Mayor Eric Garcetti in 2014. His last poetry book, *My Nature is Hunger* (Northwestern University, 2005), won the 2005 Paterson Book Award. His 1993 memoir, *Always Running: La Vida Loca: Gang Days in L.A.* (Touchstone, 2005), won various awards. Rodríguez has a dozen other books of poetry, children's literature, fiction and nonfiction. He is also founding editor of

Tía Chucha Press, now in its twenty-fifth year, and co-founder of Tía Chucha Centro Cultural & Bookstore in the San Fernando Valley. His latest book, *It Calls You Back: An Odyssey through Love, Addiction, Revolutions, and Healing* (Touchstone, 2005), was a finalist for the 2012 National Book Critics Circle Award.

Henry A. J. Ramos is an author, social justice activist and artist. Presently he serves as President & CEO of the Insight Center for Community Economic Development, a leading national economic policy think tank focused on promoting asset building and economic security in diverse, low-income communities. He is also past executive editor of the Arte Público Press Hispanic Civil Rights Series and founding editor of the *Harvard Journal of Hispanic Policy* at Harvard University's John F. Kennedy School of Government. He is the author of *The American G.I. Forum: In Pursuit of the Dream, 1948–1983* (Arte Público Press, 1998).

Chaplain Javier Stauring is Co–Director of the Office of Restorative Justice of the Archdiocese of Los Angeles. Javier is also Director for Healing Justice Coalition, an interfaith coalition of faith-based organizations in California who are involved in juvenile justice reform. In 2007 Javier was appointed by Governor Schwarzenegger to the Juvenile Justice State Commission and contributed to the publication of the "Juvenile Justice Operational Master Plan—Blueprint for an Outcome Oriented Juvenile Justice System." Javier was honored by Human Rights Watch for his work on behalf of incarcerated young people.

Jerry Tello is an internationally recognized expert and trainer in the areas of fatherhood, family strengthening and community peace. As co-founder of the National Compadres Network and the present Director of the National Latino Fatherhood and Family Institute, he has authored several books addressing the issues of fatherhood, male rites of passage, gang violence prevention, teen pregnancy prevention and family well-being. Tello has received numerous awards, including the Ambassador of Peace Award and Presidential Crime Victims Service Award.